Hot Drinks
for Cold Nights

Hot Drinks
for Cold Nights

GREAT HOT CHOCOLATES, TASTY TEAS *&* COZY COFFEE DRINKS

LIANA KRISSOFF PHOTOGRAPHS BY KIRSTEN STRECKER

Stewart, Tabori *&* Chang • New York

Published in 2005 by
Stewart, Tabori & Chang
115 West 18th Street
New York, NY 10011
www.abramsbooks.com

Library of Congress Cataloging-in-Publication Data
Krissoff, Liana.
  Hot drinks for cold nights : great hot chocolates, tasy teas & cozy
coffee drinks / Liana Krissoff; photographs by Kirsten Strecker.
    p. cm.
  Includes index.
  ISBN 1-58479-440-2
  1. Beverages. 2. Cocoa. I. Title.

TX815.K75 2005
  641.8'75--dc22   2005028969

Printed in China by C&C Offset Printing Co., Ltd.

10 9 8 7 6 5 4 3 2 1
First Printing

Stewart, Tabori & Chang is a subsidiary of

ACKNOWLEDGMENTS

Thanks first must go to Marisa Bulzone, my editor, and the rest of the crack team who helped to put this book together: Kirsten Strecker and Heather Ann Thomas; Michael Pederson, Tracy Harlor, and Darius Marter; Lynda White; Julie Hoffer; and Leda Scheintaub.

I'd also like to thank the many people who have cooked and talked with me about food and drink over the years, especially my mom, Diana Fredley, who in addition to teaching me most of what I know about food has always been ready with a much-too-long and ridiculously involved answer to every dumb question I've called her with since I left home—her influence can be seen in every recipe here. Finally I'd like to thank my exceptionally game husband, Derek, for his patience and unfailing love even in the face of early-morning hot toddies and late-night espressos.

CONTENTS

Introduction   8

Great Hot Chocolates   21

BASIC HOT CHOCOLATE

PEPPERMINT-STUFFED MARSHMALLOWS

BASIC HOT COCOA

4 A.M. IN MADRID: *CHURROS Y CHOCOLATE*

ORANGE-SCENTED HOT CHOCOLATE

ARBOL CHILE HOT COCOA

GUAVA AND *QUESO FRESCO* TURNOVERS

BASIL-MINT HOT CHOCOLATE

EARL GREY–SCENTED HOT CHOCOLATE

SAFFRON-ORANGE WHITE CHOCOLATE

CHOCOLATE-DIPPED ORANGE CANDIES

ROSE FLOWER WHITE CHOCOLATE

MEXICAN HOT CHOCOLATE TWO WAYS

ALMOND HOT COCOA

CACAO NIB MASA DRINK

Tasty Teas   51

BASIC CHAI TEA

GREEN TEA "CAPPUCCINO"

TOASTED BARLEY TEA

HOLIDAY SPICED TEA

HOT TODDY

LYCHEE BLACK TEA WITH CHERRY WINE

SAKE *&* PEAR OOLONG TEA

HONEYED TISANE

CANDIED LAVENDER BLOSSOMS

PERSIMMON, BLACK PEPPERCORN *&* GINGER TEA

PERSIMMON TEACAKE

CINNAMON-CHILE INFUSION WITH DRIED JUJUBES

Cozy Coffee Drinks   77 | BASIC CAPPUCCINO
KOREATOWN CUBAN COFFEE
CAFÉ MOCHA WITH COFFEE WHIPPED CREAM
WALNUT-CHERRY BISCOTTI
CHICORY COFFEE
REAL IRISH COFFEE
HOT PENNY RUM
COFFEE GROG
SWISS COFFEE COCKTAIL
CAFÉ BRÛLOT WITH CINNAMON CREAM
SWEETENED ESPRESSO WITH GRAPPA
CRUNCHY ESPRESSO-BEAN CHOCOLATES
MELYA

GLÜGG
Drinks to Warm   107 | MULLED WINE
Body & Soul   MULLED WHITE WINE WITH PEACH JUICE
HOT BUTTERED BOURBON
SPICED CANDIED NUTS
CLASSIC MULLED CIDER
BLACK CHERRY CIDER
HOT BENEFACTOR
HOT MILK PUNCH
DUTCH WARM MILK
WARM BRANDY FLIP

Metric Conversion Chart   128

Sources   129

Index   132

INTRODUCTION

Nothing warms you on a cold winter night like a mug of steaming coffee taken in front of the fireplace—unless it's a cup of lemony hot tea sipped under the covers, or a pan of sweet and dark hot cocoa simmering on the stove, homemade marshmallows at the ready. The basic coffee, tea, and chocolate drinks will never let you down: They're easy, quick, and satisfying. But you might occasionally have a taste for something different, new—and that's when this book will come in handy.

Here I offer variations on the classic hot drinks from around the world—Korea to Spain, Mexico to the Netherlands. I've taken advantage of some of the unusual ingredients that are becoming more common in good supermarkets and specialty foods stores—cacao nibs, for example, dried jujubes, and lychee black tea—but have also tried to develop drinks that can be made anywhere, by anyone. Some of the drinks are alcoholic, but you won't find any of the corny hot cocktail recipes that fill other hot-drinks books here—no banana liqueur, not even any hazelnut syrup, has made its way into this book. It's not that I don't appreciate those kinds of drinks, but that there were so many other, more sophisticated hot drinks I wanted to include: I think you'll enjoy trying drinks like the elegant Earl Grey hot chocolate on page 35, the toasted barley tea on page 60, the coffee grog with spiced butter on page 96, and the warm milk with anise sugar cubes on page 122.

Most of the recipes in this book can be prepared using only the most basic kitchen appliances and utensils, but there are some specialized tools that will make preparing and serving these hot drinks easier —or at least ones that will make certain drinks more authentic. For details about how to use these tools, see the introductions to each of the following three chapters.

Coffee and Espresso Makers

Manual Drip Coffee Maker: A manual drip pot is simply a cone-shaped filter holder that attaches to or rests atop a pot: Hot water is poured from a teakettle over the coffee in the filter, and coffee flows down into the pot. Try to find one with an insulated carafe for a pot, and a filter holder that attaches securely to the pot so there's no danger it'll tip off.

Electric Drip Coffee Maker: Electric coffee makers are available in every price range, and are outfitted with everything from digital timers and radios to built-in ion-exchange water filters and burr coffee grinders. And every manufacturer, it seems, touts its own revolutionary advance in coffee brewing. If expense is not an issue, I'd suggest an electric coffee maker with a thermal carafe pot rather than a glass pot that sits on a hot burner. Even after just 10 minutes on a burner, coffee can begin to taste scorched and sour.

Neapolitan Flip Pot: When purchasing a Neapolitan flip pot, in which coffee is brewed by the drip method on the stovetop, skip the inexpensive ones made out of flimsy stainless steel or aluminum. I've used several of these cheap pots, and the mess they make is not worth the (admittedly very little) trouble of using them. Should you be lucky enough to find an old one (it might have a metal rather than plastic handle), or should you have the resources to splurge on a very pricey one, you'll be well rewarded with a coffee pot for life: easy to use, easy to clean, and nearly indestructible.

Vietnamese Filter: These little stainless-steel contraptions cost about three bucks apiece at Asian markets and grocery stores; because each can be used for only one cup of coffee at a time, you need to buy as many filter sets as people you want to serve.

French Press: Try to find a French press that's insulated in some way rather than one of just plain glass, which doesn't retain the coffee's heat for very long. If you can't find a thermal French press, consider using a small one that makes only enough coffee as you and yours can drink right away. Some French presses, such as that made by Bonjour, now have a solid metal sliding disk above the screen mesh that you can close when the coffee has brewed for the correct amount of time to avoid overextraction of the grounds. Finally, look for one with a fine screen in the spout to filter out any grounds that might have made it through the mesh plunger.

Turkish Ibrik: A basic *ibrik*, made of heavy stainless steel, with a long plastic handle, costs about twelve dollars and can be found at international foods stores and kitchenware shops. Fancier ones made of elaborately molded copper or brass, with more pronounced "waists," are a little harder to come by—check with local or online coffee merchants. *Ibriks* are also excellent pots for warming milk or melting butter on the stovetop.

Macchineta: This small, simple aluminum stovetop espresso maker will set you back about fifteen dollars, though the sleeker, larger, or more complex designs will run quite a bit more—as much as sixty or seventy dollars.

Electric Espresso Machine: The holy grail of the espresso enthusiast is the near-commercial-quality home espresso machine. It would be nice to be able to write that there's a decent one available in every price range; the truth is, real espresso is going to cost you, because the only electric machines that can produce the amount of pressure needed to brew the best espresso (about 9 bars of pressure) are ones that are pump-driven (cheap steam-driven machines can produce only about 3 bars of pressure). In a pump-driven espresso machine, water is pumped from a reservoir into a boiler, where it's heated rapidly almost to boiling, then forced through the espresso grounds at high pressure. Some higher-end machines have two boilers, one for heating water for espresso and one that heats water to be used for steaming milk with the frothing wand; using a single-boiler machine, you might have to wait awhile for the boiler to reheat after pulling a shot of espresso before steaming the milk for cappuccino. Superautomatic pump espresso machines that grind, dose, and tamp the espresso grounds, then brew exactly the amount of espresso you've digitally programmed it to produce can be extremely expensive. They are also, however, convenient and easy to use.

If a good pump-driven espresso machine is out of your price range (or if you don't have room for a huge machine on your kitchen counter), a *macchineta* is your best alternative when making the espresso recipes in this book: The stovetop espresso pot will produce a far better cup than any cheap steam-driven electric espresso machine.

Coffee Grinders and Spice Mills

My old rotary-blade coffee grinder/spice mill has worked brilliantly for about ten years, during which I have ground coffee beans at least once a day, every day, and occasionally subjected the little machine to whole cinnamon sticks, allspice berries, and fenugreek. Despite the abuse, and despite a slight dulling of the blades, it still does the job—though it now takes about twice as long to get coffee as finely ground as it used to when it was new. I was almost sad when I had the opportunity to replace it with a fancy new burr coffee grinder (the old grinder has been demoted to spice mill), but in truth the burr grinder is an absolute dream. To grind coffee finely or coarsely, rather than running the machine for a longer or shorter period of time, you simply turn the knob to tighten or loosen the burr grinding mechanism: This reduces the time that the beans are in contact with the metal (in a rotary grinder the coffee beans can get warm from the friction before they're fully ground, resulting in a loss of flavor), and ensures that all the beans are ground evenly—no big chunks among the espresso grounds. Stand-alone burr grinders are widely available, and many electric coffee makers now come equipped with good burr grinders that portion the grounds directly into the filter for immediate brewing.

Cleaning a Coffee Grinder: To clean a coffee or spice grinder, wash and thoroughly dry the lid, and wipe out the inside of the grinder with a paper towel. Put a couple tablespoons of granulated sugar in the grinder and run the motor until the sugar is very finely powdered, then dump out the sugar and wipe out the lid and inside of the grinder with a paper towel. Repeat until no trace of ground coffee or spice remains.

TEAKETTLES

If you drink a lot of tea, an electric teakettle is a great convenience, but a good stovetop kettle, either made of solid copper (often these are lined with nickel) or with a copper bottom, can heat water to a boil almost as quickly. Models with copper coils at the bottom, designed to be used on gas burners, heat water even more efficiently. When choosing a stovetop teakettle, make sure it is comfortable in your hand as you lift the cap and pour—I've noticed that many of the more handsome designs are decidedly unergonomic.

Tea Strainers and Infusers: A simple, small fine-mesh strainer will work just fine for making the drinks in this book, but if your concerns run more to the aesthetic, a perforated silver-plated strainer with a separate drip bowl would beautifully complement an heirloom English tea set. Cone-shaped Chinese bamboo strainers also do a fine job.

Tea balls and infusers, which hold the tea leaves so that they can be easily fished out of the teapot when the steeping time is up, should be small enough to fit down in your teapot but large enough to allow the leaves to float freely when the ball is submerged in the water. If you find that the leaves are packed tightly inside when you open up the tea ball to empty it, the ball is too small for the amount of tea you're using.

TEAPOTS AND CUPS

There are scores of varieties of teapots, the vessels in which tea is served. Most teapots are also brewing containers, and some kinds also serve as teakettles for heating the water itself.

English: The classic English earthenware teapot is nearly spherical, with a spout and lid. The simpler the shape, and the closer it is to perfectly round, the easier it is to clean, and spherical pots also seem to retain heat better than odd-shaped ones. Often the pot comes with an infuser, which rests inside the top opening under the lid and holds loose tea leaves so that they can be lifted out of the water and discarded as soon as the tea has brewed for the proper amount of time. An infuser insert eliminates the need for a tea ball (or a strainer to remove the leaves as the tea is poured from the pot into individual serving cups), and gives the tea leaves plenty of space to expand as the tea brews. The inserts may be of the same material as the teapot, or they may be made of stainless-steel mesh.

Clear glass teapots in the English style usually come with infuser inserts, or with a strainer built into the base of the spout. They're the ideal containers for brewing flower teas, or teas that are gathered and tied into shapes that unfold into beautiful forms as the leaves absorb water; remove the infuser before brewing these special teas so that the flowers and tea can expand without impediment.

Cups and saucers for English-style tea service, of course, vary dramatically in style. Because English tea is generally consumed while still quite hot, the cups should have a handle in a design that allows room for you to grasp it securely without burning your fingers on the side of the cup.

Japanese Cast-Iron: The most common and practical Japanese teapot is the *tetsubin*, a small cast-iron vessel with, usually, a stainless-steel mesh infuser for leaf (not powdered) tea. The inside of the pot, apart from the spout, is glazed; the iron of the spout is left exposed so that trace amounts of iron may be picked up as the hot tea is poured out—enhancing the tea's flavor and adding an essential mineral to the diet.

Cast-iron handleless cups, usually of 2-ounce capacity and glazed on the inside, are the traditional accompaniment to a *tetsubin*, and cast-iron or bamboo serving trivets are also widely available (a raftlike trivet for a *tetsubin* is easy to make yourself with a few dozen short lengths of bamboo and some raffia to bind them together).

Chinese Clay: Clay *yixing* teapots are usually very small, suitable for just one or two servings of fine tea, with an interior of unglazed, porous clay. Tannins in the tea seep into the clay, effectively "curing" the pot (which should never be washed, just rinsed). Over time and with regular use, the seasoned clay will impart the flavor of the tea to the hot water even if no new tea leaves have been added. For this reason, only one kind of tea should be used in each clay pot, to avoid mixing the flavors of different teas.

Tiny (2-ounce or smaller) handleless clay cups, along with a large bowl for rinsing and preheating the *yixing* pots, complete a basic Chinese tea set.

Manual and Electric Milk Frothers

What fun little toys are milk frothers! Whether you go for the classic manual frother, which looks like a small French press coffee maker with its glass or plastic beaker and mesh plunger screen, or the sleek and vaguely

sinister-looking battery-powered frother with its tiny, insectoid coil whisk and pod-shaped handle, you'll only be out about twenty dollars. Each works as well as the other to aerate milk (full-fat to skim are frothable), and despite what the directions say, I've found that preheated milk froths just as easily and quickly as cold milk using these frothers. A manual frother must be used with the glass container it comes with, which means that only a small amount of milk can be frothed at a time; also, if you prefer to heat the milk after it's been frothed, as recommended by most manufacturers, note that the beaker might not fit upright in your microwave oven. The handheld electric frothers can foam up hot or cold milk in just about any container. It's possible to whip heavy cream using either gadget, but it won't have the fluffy, light consistency of conventionally whipped cream—it'll be thicker and denser.

Immersion or stick blenders usually come with a cream-whipping disk attachment, making it the ideal tool for larger batches of whipped heavy cream—especially if you'd prefer not to dirty a handheld or stand mixer (or if it's already in use).

Blenders

I use either a heavy-duty blender to puree fruit (with a little water) for teas and hot punches, and for making quick, frothy Mexican-style hot chocolate. For smaller batches, an immersion (stick) blender works well: For the pear juice in the Sake and Pear Oolong Tea (page 66), for example, you can just blend chopped and cored or pitted fruit—pears, plums, peaches, lychee—in a sturdy tall plastic mixing cup (many immersion blenders come with one for making milkshakes and smoothies), then push the puree and juice through a sieve and discard the solids and use the puree instead of bottled juice.

Coffee and Tea Esoterica

Part of the allure of making coffee and tea is the feeling that you're engaging in some sort of ancient ritual. And nothing says ritual like antique silver sugar-cube tongs. Or a handcrafted ceramic teapot drip-catcher. Or an inlaid-wood tea chest. Or a rosewood-handled espresso tamper. Or a coffee measuring scoop that's slightly smaller than an espresso measuring scoop, (if you're thinking you should have one of each, you're a true collector).

Nonstick Saucepans

When making hot drinks that require heating milk on the stovetop—hot chocolate and cocoa, especially—a nonstick surface is a godsend. If you've ever tried to scrub a layer of accidentally scalded milk off the bottom of a stainless-steel pan, you'll understand the value of infused anodized aluminum. A 2-quart nonstick saucepan is perfect for most of the recipes in this book.

Nonstick Whisks

To avoid damaging nonstick saucepans, you should use only nonstick (silicone-coated) whisks to make these drinks. A small nonstick balloon whisk is good for maximum aeration of, say, hot chocolate drinks, and a nonstick flat sauce whisk or spiral (coil) whisk is practically essential for getting into the corners of the saucepan in order to incorporate all the ingredients evenly.

MOLINILLOS

The *molinillo*, an intricately turned and carved wood whisk used to beat hot chocolate to a thick but light froth, was invented by the Spanish colonists of Mexico in the eighteenth century to froth hot chocolate drinks (indigenous Mexicans would aerate their chocolate drinks by pouring the liquid back and forth between two pitchers, which required much more skill than using a *molinillo*). Special glazed clay and porcelain chocolate pots were made to accommodate the bulb-shaped *molinillos*, but you can easily use a *molinillo* in a narrow saucepan—as long as the liquid is deep enough to cover most of the wide portion of the *molinillo*. A regular balloon whisk, it must be said, works just as well to froth hot chocolate (and is easier to clean).

HEATPROOF GLASSWARE

Almost all of the drinks in this book are meant to be served in heatproof mugs or cups, Irish-coffee glasses, or hot-toddy mugs. Some of the warm (rather than hot) drinks, such as the flips, can be served in regular glassware without risk. If you're not absolutely sure that the vessel you're pouring a hot drink into is heatproof, take two precautions: Preheat the cup by filling it with hot tap water before emptying it and pouring in the hot drink, and put a silver spoon in the cup before you fill it with the hot drink—the silver absorbs some of the heat from the liquid and prevents the cup or glass from cracking.

GREAT HOT CHOCOLATES

Making the Perfect Hot Chocolate

I had always thought that the world's chocolate-drinking population could be divided into devotees of hot chocolate and the partisans of the hot cocoa camp. I'd long been a loyal campaigner in the latter group, unable to understand how anyone wouldn't prefer the dark, thin acidity of the hot drink made with cocoa to the sweet, thick richness of the one made with melted chocolate. And my mom never made hot chocolate—always cocoa. But after experimenting with different chocolates and sweetnesses, and using various combinations of milk and cream, I came to appreciate the sensations offered by good hot chocolate just as much as the beloved cocoa of my childhood. I have even come to like the much-maligned white chocolate—and all it took to convert me was a pound of Callebaut, the fine Belgian chocolate, which I consumed in about three days. I have discovered that as long as your ingredients are good, your utensils nonstick, and your technique sound, it's possible to make either hot chocolate or hot cocoa to suit your taste or mood, as the proportions of all the ingredients can be easily varied.

Ingredients

Solid Chocolate: When developing and testing these recipes, I used Callebaut and Valrhona bittersweet chocolate that contained 64 to 66 percent cocoa. These are European chocolates that are readily available in the United States and I highly recommend either. The rule of thumb: When choosing bittersweet chocolate for hot drinks, use one that you wouldn't mind eating plain. If using white chocolate, check the label to make sure that what you're buying contains cocoa butter.

Page 20
Basic Hot Chocolate
and Peppermint-Stuffed
Marshmallows

Cocoa Powder: Always use pure unsweetened cocoa powder—that means cocoa solids with no sugar or other flavorings added. Unlike baking, when making hot cocoa it doesn't much matter whether you use natural or Dutch-process (alkalized) cocoa powder. Dutch-process powder tends to be less lumpy, which is nice, and darker, which is nicer. But if you use a good-quality nonalkalized cocoa powder you won't notice much difference between that and alkalized. I use Ghirardelli (natural) unsweetened cocoa powder.

Milk and cream: In the basic recipes that follow, I use a combination of whole milk and half-and-half; in others, a combination of whole milk and cream is specified. The given proportions will yield what I find to be the most desirable consistency for each specific drink. Of course you can play with the fat content of the dairy in your hot chocolates and cocoas all you want. As long as you keep the total amount of dairy the same as in the recipe, you'll still end up with an excellent drink.

Sugar: The easiest way to sweeten hot chocolate is by using solid chocolate that already has enough sugar added to yield the sweetness you want. For me, this is a very dark bittersweet chocolate—again, Valrhona and Callebaut (60 to 70 percent cocoa) are both excellent. The tinkerers among us might be most happy using unsweetened chocolate and adding sugar to the milk as it heats, or sweetening with honey or brown sugar. (Using brown sugar instead of white granulated sugar makes almost no difference in the flavor of the finished hot cocoa or chocolate, except that for some reason you need to use a little more brown sugar to get the same amount of sweetness.)

Flavorings and Extras: A touch of vanilla adds depth to the flavor of the chocolate, and a bit of salt accents the sweetness of the drink. Mexican chocolate is usually flavored with cinnamon or canela, chiles, and vanilla, and the Spanish also flavored chocolate with allspice when the Aztec first introduced them to cacao in the sixteenth century.

TECHNIQUE

Hot Chocolate: There are several ways to make hot chocolate, and these recipes reflect those different techniques. As described in the basic recipe (page 28), heat the liquid (milk and half-and-half) and sweetener in a saucepan (nonstick is best; see page 18) to almost a simmer, then remove the pan from the heat and whisk in finely chopped chocolate (again using a nonstick whisk; see page 18), whisking until it's completely melted. If the chocolate is not chopped finely enough, and you find yourself left with little bits of unmelted chocolate after a minute or so of whisking, just return the pan to very low heat and cook until the milk is almost at a simmer and the chocolate is thoroughly incorporated; do not let it boil or you'll scald the milk and the chocolate will become bitter.

You can also melt the chocolate before adding it to the milk and sweetener. While the milk mixture is heating, put chopped chocolate in a bowl over a pan of simmering water and stir occasionally with a rubber spatula until it's just about melted, then scrape it into the milk mixture and whisk to combine. This will yield a smooth, silky hot chocolate every time, but of course it requires an extra pan and a bowl.

Finally, there's the blender method. Put the chocolate, chopped or not, in a blender and pour in the hot steaming milk and sweetener mixture. Blend for about 30 seconds, until the chocolate is melted and

A variety of chocolate forms and flavorings. Clockwise from top: hard chocolate, cocoa powder, cacao nibs, cinnamon, vanilla extract, and rose flower water. At left, a whisk and a molinillo.

Chocolate

the drink is frothy (remove the insert in the lid as the blender is running to allow air into the mixture for a fluffier drink).

Hot Cocoa: There's really only one best way to make hot cocoa, and it's described in the basic recipe (page 28). Combine cocoa powder and sugar in a saucepan with a small amount of water—just enough to make a goopy paste. Heat over very low heat, stirring constantly to keep the cocoa from burning and sticking to the pan, until bubbling. Let the cocoa mixture cook at a very low simmer for 1 minute, then whisk in the cold milk mixture. Whisk vigorously to combine the milk and cocoa mixture—be sure to get that whisk in the corners of the pan and keep running it across the bottom of the pan. Cook over low heat until the hot cocoa is steaming but not boiling. Because this technique uses a bit of water in addition to the milk and half-and-half, and because cocoa has less fat in it than solid chocolate, it's not as rich and thick as hot chocolate. If you want a richer drink, use more cream and less milk than the recipe calls for.

BASIC HOT CHOCOLATE

Serves 2

1   cup whole milk
1   cup half-and-half
     Scant ¼ cup sugar
     Pinch of salt
2   ounces unsweetened
     chocolate, roughly
     chopped
½   teaspoon pure vanilla
     extract
2   large marshmallows or
     Peppermint-Stuffed
     Marshmallows

Makes 25 large marshmallows

     About ½ cup cornstarch
     About ½ cup confectioners'
     sugar
2   7-gram envelopes
     unflavored gelatin
1¼   cups granulated sugar
⅓   cup light corn syrup
2   large egg whites
½   teaspoon pure vanilla
     extract
25   disk-shaped peppermint
     hard candies

I prefer to use unsweetened chocolate and add sugar so that I can control the sweetness of the hot chocolate myself (I like it less sweet); however, you may omit the sugar and use bittersweet chocolate for a similar result. Using equal parts milk and half-and-half results in an extremely rich drink, as most of the hot-chocolate lovers I know prefer, but feel free to use more milk and less half-and-half.

In a 2-quart nonstick saucepan, combine the milk, half-and-half, sugar, and salt and place over low heat until steaming and just starting to bubble around the edge of the pan. Add the chocolate and bring just to a simmer, whisking until the chocolate is completely melted, about 2 minutes; do not let the mixture boil. Stir in the vanilla and pour into 2 warmed mugs. Top each with a marshmallow and serve immediately.

Peppermint-Stuffed Marshmallows

In winter, my parents would make hot cocoa topped with big marshmallows (giving my dad a ready excuse to mourn the passing of his beloved individually wrapped Campfires), and at Christmastime my brother and I would be allowed to stir the whole mess with a candy cane. Here I've combined the two candies into one, so they melt together into the chocolate.

Heavily dust an 8½- or 9-inch square silicone cake pan with equal parts of some of the cornstarch and confectioners' sugar (if using a nonstick aluminum pan, first grease it lightly with vegetable shortening, then dust it).

In a large mixing bowl, soften the gelatin in ⅓ cup cold water. Set aside.

In a small saucepan, combine $1/3$ cup water, the granulated sugar, and corn syrup, place over low heat, and stir until the sugar is dissolved. Raise the heat to medium and bring to a boil; cook at a boil until the syrup reaches 240°F on a candy thermometer (soft-ball stage). Slowly pour the syrup into the gelatin mixture, stirring until combined; it will bubble up quite a bit and then the foam will recede. Using an electric stand mixer, beat on high speed until the mixture is thick, tripled in volume, glossy, and bright white, about 8 minutes; the mixture will be very sticky, and might work its way up the beaters toward the end of the beating time—this is okay. Set aside.

In a separate medium mixing bowl, using very clean beaters, beat the egg whites until they hold stiff peaks. Fold the egg whites, along with the vanilla, into the gelatin mixture until just combined and smooth. Scrape the mixture into the prepared pan and smooth the surface. Working quickly so that you finish before the marshmallow begins to set, place the candies in rows on the surface of the marshmallow, pressing them into the mixture. Use a spatula to gently spread marshmallow mixture over the top of each candy.

Chill in the refrigerator for at least 4 hours, until set and firm. Run a thin knife around the edges of the pan to loosen the marshmallow. Heavily dust a work surface with equal parts cornstarch and confectioners' sugar and turn the marshmallow out of the pan. Using a sharp knife dipped in cold water, cut into 25 squares. (To avoid cutting into the hidden candies, gently press down on the top of the marshmallow with your finger to feel where they are.) Dust again with more cornstarch and confectioners' sugar, shaking off the excess. Store in the refrigerator, in an airtight container in one layer or stacked between sheets of wax paper; the marshmallows will keep for about 1 week.

BASIC HOT COCOA

Serves 2

½ cup pure unsweetened
 cocoa powder
2 tablespoons sugar
 Pinch of salt
1½ cups whole milk
½ cup half-and-half
½ teaspoon vanilla extract

This proportion of whole milk and half-and-half will yield quite a rich hot cocoa; unless I'm making it for company, I'll usually just use skim milk (which is what I prefer to drink straight) and add just a touch of half-and-half (which my husband keeps in stock for his coffee).

In a 2-quart nonstick saucepan, whisk together the cocoa powder, sugar, and salt. Whisk in ½ cup water and place the pan over very low heat. Cook, stirring, until the mixture is smooth and starts to bubble, about 3 minutes. Whisk in the milk and half-and-half and cook, whisking frequently, until the mixture just comes to a simmer but is not boiling. Add the vanilla, whisk again, then remove from the heat and pour the cocoa into 2 warmed mugs or cups. Serve immediately.

The Chocolate Skin

You either love it or hate it—the skin that inevitably forms on the surface of hot chocolate and cocoa as it begins to cool in your mug. If you hate it, the best you can do is delay its appearance, and there are a couple ways to do that. First, the frothier the top of the drink is, the less likely it is that a skin will be able to form before you finish your mugful: Use a good balloon whisk to froth the hot chocolate right before pouring it into mugs, or run an electric milk frother through it for ten or twenty seconds. Second, I think that maybe, just maybe, marshmallows were invented for the express purpose of covering the top of hot chocolate to keep it from solidifying.

4 A.M. IN MADRID: *Churros y Chocolate*

Serves 4 to 6

½ cup pure unsweetened
    cocoa powder

1 tablespoon cornstarch

⅓ to ½ cup sugar, to taste

2 cups whole milk

½ teaspoon pure vanilla
    extract

    Churros (page 33)

Madrid's answer to Paris's late-night bowl of French onion soup is this thick, very rich chocolate, into which sugary fried churros *are to be dipped.*

In a 2-quart nonstick saucepan, whisk together the cocoa powder, cornstarch, sugar, and ½ cup water until smooth. Whisk in the milk, place over medium-low heat, and bring just to a slow simmer; simmer for about 2 minutes, whisking frequently, until the chocolate is thick and glossy and smooth, like a runny pudding. Add the vanilla, whisk again, then remove from the heat and pour into small cups. Serve immediately with *churros* for dipping.

CHURROS

Makes 16 to 20

2 tablespoons unsalted butter

1 tablespoon sugar, plus ¼ cup for dusting

Pinch of salt

1 cup all-purpose flour, sifted

3 large eggs

Vegetable oil for frying

Put 1 cup water, the butter, 1 tablespoon sugar, and the salt in a 2-quart saucepan and place over medium-high heat; cook, stirring to combine, until the butter is melted and the water is foaming up in the pan. Remove from the heat and immediately add the flour all at once. Stir with a wooden spoon until the mixture forms a smooth ball. One at a time, add the eggs, stirring vigorously until the dough is shaggy and each egg has been completely combined before adding the next egg.

Heat 1 inch of oil in a heavy pot over medium-high heat until it reaches 375°F.

Put the dough in a heavy-duty (cloth) pastry bag fitted with a #849 closed star tip (about 1³/₈ inches wide at the base). Using one hand to squeeze the pastry bag and the other hand to cut the dough off at the end with a butter knife, carefully pipe 2- to 3-inch lengths of dough into the hot oil, a few at a time. Use tongs to turn the *churros* constantly so that they cook evenly. When they are deep brown all over, in 2 to 2½ minutes, remove the *churros* with the tongs and place them on several layers of paper bags to drain. Repeat with the remaining dough. Toss the hot *churros* with the ¼ cup sugar to coat thoroughly, then serve warm.

ORANGE-SCENTED HOT CHOCOLATE

Serves 2

3   ounces bittersweet
    chocolate

2   cups whole milk

3   tablespoons heavy cream

4   4-inch strips orange zest,
    removed with a vegetable
    peeler

    Barely Sweetened
    Whipped Cream

Makes enough for 4 servings

1   cup cold heavy cream

1   teaspoon confectioners'
    sugar

For a more intense orange flavor, let the zest steep in the milk for 5 minutes, then whisk and reheat before pouring it over the chopped chocolate.

Finely chop the chocolate and put it in a medium heatproof bowl. In a 2-quart nonstick saucepan over low heat, combine the milk, cream, and orange zest and bring just to a boil. Pour the mixture over the chocolate and whisk until the chocolate is melted and smooth. Discard the orange zest. Pour the hot chocolate into 2 warmed mugs, dollop with the whipped cream, and serve immediately.

Barely Sweetened Whipped Cream

Pour the cream into a chilled stainless-steel bowl and add the confectioners' sugar. With a chilled balloon whisk or an immersion (stick) blender fitted with the cream-whipping attachment, whip the cream until soft but not stiff peaks form.

EARL GREY–SCENTED HOT CHOCOLATE

Serves 3 or 4

1½ cups whole milk

2 tablespoons heavy cream

1½ teaspoons Earl Grey tea leaves

3 ounces good-quality bittersweet chocolate, finely chopped

Use your best dark bittersweet chocolate (at least 60 percent cocoa) for this silky, smoky hot chocolate, and serve it in tiny teacups or demitasse cups. The fat in the chocolate and cream makes the drink feel almost mousselike in your mouth, and then suddenly the acidity of the tea cuts through as you swallow it.

In a 2-quart nonstick saucepan over medium-low heat, combine the milk and cream and bring almost to a boil. Remove from the heat and stir in the tea leaves. Cover and set aside to steep for 4 minutes. Pour through a fine-mesh sieve into a clean nonstick saucepan and discard the tea leaves. Place the milk mixture over low heat. Add the chocolate and cook, whisking constantly, until the chocolate is melted and the mixture is smooth and foamy but not boiling. Pour into demitasse cups and serve immediately.

ARBOL CHILE HOT COCOA

Serves 2

½ cup pure unsweetened
   cocoa powder

2 tablespoons sugar

⅛ teaspoon arbol chile
   powder (see Note), plus
   a pinch for garnish

   Pinch of salt

1 cup whole milk

1 cup half-and-half
   Barely Sweetened
   Whipped Cream (page
   34; optional)

Renowned chocolatier Jacques Torres famously serves a very thick, rich chile-spiced hot chocolate at his café and chocolate shop in Brooklyn, but Central and South Americans have been using chiles in hot chocolate for centuries. My version is less dense and much less sweet than Torres's, but just as intensely chocolatey.

In a 2-quart nonstick saucepan, whisk together the cocoa powder, sugar, chile powder, and salt. Whisk in ½ cup water and place the pan over very low heat. Cook, stirring, until the mixture is smooth and starts to bubble, about 3 minutes. Whisk in the milk and half-and-half and cook, whisking frequently, until the mixture just comes to a simmer but is not boiling. Whisk again, then remove from the heat and pour the cocoa into 2 warmed mugs or cups. Top with the whipped cream and sprinkle with just a tiny pinch of chile powder, if desired, and serve immediately.

Note: Freshly ground whole dried chiles are best: Use a coffee or spice mill (page 11) to pulverize them as finely as possible, then shake the powder through a fine-mesh sieve and discard or regrind the larger pieces. You can also use ground cayenne pepper, but if it's preground it won't be nearly as spicy or deeply flavorful, so use a touch more.

GUAVA AND QUESO FRESCO TURNOVERS

Makes about 32 small turnovers

For the pastry dough:
3   cups all-purpose flour
½   teaspoon salt
1¼ cups vegetable shortening
1   large egg, lightly beaten
1   tablespoon vinegar
4 to 5 tablespoons ice water

For the turnovers:
6   ounces guava paste
     (see Notes), sliced
     ⅛ inch thick
6   ounces *queso fresco*
     (see Notes), sliced
     ⅛ inch thick

This is a good way to use leftover pastry dough. If I'm making a single-crust pie or tart, I go ahead and make enough dough for a double-crust pie (the quantity in this recipe) and freeze half of it for these guava turnovers, something quick and sweet to go with, say, a winter-afternoon spicy hot chocolate, or an ill-advised late-evening espresso.

Preheat the oven to 375°F.

Make the pastry dough: In a large bowl, combine the flour and salt. Using a pastry cutter, cut in the shortening until the mixture resembles coarse meal. Make a well in the center and add the egg, vinegar, and 4 tablespoons of the water. Use a fork to beat the egg and toss all the ingredients together gently, then use your hands to gather the dough into a rough ball, adding more water if necessary. Turn the dough out onto a lightly floured work surface. With the palm of your hand, smear the ball flat onto the work surface, then use a bench knife to scrape the dough back into a rough ball. Repeat, but don't overwork the dough or knead it. Divide the dough into two equal balls, wrap them in plastic, and chill in the refrigerator for 30 minutes or up to 1 day (you can also freeze the dough, well wrapped, for several months; thaw in the refrigerator).

Roll one ball of dough out to ⅛ inch thick on a floured work surface using a floured or nonstick rolling pin. Cut out circles using a 2-inch round or fluted cookie cutter.

Make the turnovers: Place a slice of guava paste and a slice of *queso fresco* on one half of each circle of dough. Fold the circle over and crimp the edges together using your fingers and the tines of a fork. Transfer to baking sheets lined with parchment paper. Reroll the scraps of dough, cut into circles, and fill. Repeat with the second ball of dough and the remaining guava paste and *queso fresco*.

Bake for 20 to 25 minutes, until the turnovers are puffy and golden brown. Remove to wire racks to cool slightly. Serve warm or at room temperature. Store leftovers in an airtight container for up to 2 days; they can be reheated and refreshed in a 375°F oven.

Notes: Guava paste can be found in Hispanic grocery stores, and often in the international-foods section of regular supermarkets. Queso fresco *is also available in Hispanic grocery stores and in supermarkets, or you can substitute fresh mozzarella.*

SAFFRON-ORANGE WHITE CHOCOLATE

Serves 2

1½ cups whole milk

½ cup heavy cream

2 cinnamon sticks, or ⅛ teaspoon ground cinnamon

Zest of ½ large orange, in 1 or 2 pieces, removed with a vegetable peeler

Good pinch of saffron threads (about ¼ teaspoon)

1½ ounces white chocolate, chopped

If you take the extra step of frothing the hot white chocolate just before serving, this extravagant, creamy yellow drink becomes even more luxurious-feeling on the palate. The delicate flavor of the saffron reveals itself just after you've swallowed.

In a 2-quart nonstick saucepan, combine the milk, cream, cinnamon, orange zest, and saffron. Place over very low heat and bring just to a simmer, then cover the pan and remove from the heat; let the milk mixture infuse for 10 minutes. Discard the cinnamon sticks and orange zest and add the white chocolate. Whisk to combine, and place over very low heat, whisking constantly, until the white chocolate is just melted and heated through. If desired, froth the mixture using an electric milk frother (see page 16) for just a few seconds, or use a balloon whisk to froth the milk mixture by hand. Pour into 2 warmed mugs or wide coffee cups and serve immediately.

CHOCOLATE-DIPPED ORANGE CANDIES

Makes about 4 dozen strips

2   large navel oranges with thick skin

1½ cups sugar

3   ounces unsweetened chocolate, chopped

Using a sharp paring knife, score the orange peel lengthwise into ½-inch-wide sections, then use your fingers to peel off the rind in strips. Trim off most of the white pith from the inside of each strip. Cut each strip in half horizontally to make roughly triangle-shaped strips.

Put the orange strips in a medium saucepan and cover with cold water. Bring to a boil over high heat, then immediately drain in a colander. Return the strips to the pan, cover with water again, and bring to a boil; drain, then repeat the blanching process twice more. Drain the orange strips and set them aside in the colander.

In the saucepan, combine the sugar with ¾ cup water and place over high heat. Stir until the sugar dissolves, but do not stir after the mixture comes to a boil. Boil for about 8 minutes, until the syrup reaches 240°F on a candy thermometer (soft-ball stage), then carefully add the orange strips. Cook over medium-high heat for about 6 minutes, until the white sides begin to become translucent; gently separate the strips with a fork as they cook, but do not stir the syrup. Use the fork to lift the orange strips out of the syrup, letting excess syrup drain back into the pan, and place on a wire rack over a sheet of wax paper to cool completely.

When the orange strips are cool and stiff, prepare the dipping chocolate: Melt the chocolate in the top of a double boiler or in a small bowl set over a pan of simmering water. Dip the wide end of each orange strip in the chocolate and return it to the rack to drain. Transfer the strips to a sheet of wax paper and chill in the refrigerator for 30 minutes to allow the chocolate to harden. Store in an airtight container for up to 1 week.

ROSE FLOWER WHITE CHOCOLATE

Serves 2 or 3

2   ounces white chocolate

1½ cups whole milk

2   tablespoons heavy cream

⅜   teaspoon rose flower water

   Untreated fresh or dried rose petals (optional; see Note)

Finely chop the white chocolate and place it in the top of a double boiler or in a small bowl set over a pan of simmering water. When the white chocolate is almost melted, remove it from the heat and set aside.

In a 2-quart nonstick saucepan, heat the milk and cream over medium-low heat until steaming but not boiling. Add the melted chocolate and whisk to combine. Cook, whisking constantly, until the mixture is foamy and almost boiling, about 3 minutes, then whisk in the rose flower water. Pour into teacups, sprinkle each serving with a few rose petals, if desired, and serve immediately.

Note: Use rose petals from flowers sold at farmer's markets (ask the purveyor to make sure the roses haven't been treated at any time with pesticides) or from your own garden if you're one of those brave souls growing roses organically.

MEXICAN HOT CHOCOLATE TWO WAYS

Serves 2

4   wedges (1½ ounces)
     Mexican chocolate, such
     as Ibarra
2   cups whole milk
     Pinch of salt

Quick & Easy

Most Mexican chocolate is flavored with artificial cinnamon flavoring, and is quite sweet. You can find it in Latin American groceries or in the Mexican foods section of some supermarkets. The traditional drink is light and airy when made in a blender, and has just a hint of chocolate flavor.

Put the chocolate in a blender and set aside. In a 2-quart nonstick saucepan, heat the milk and salt over low heat until the milk is bubbling around the edges and almost at a simmer. Pour the milk into the blender and blend until the chocolate is melted and the mixture is foamy and light. Pour into 2 warmed mugs and serve immediately.

Serves 4

4   cups whole milk
2   cinnamon sticks
¼   vanilla bean, split
     Pinch of salt
2   ounces semisweet
     chocolate, finely chopped

Special-Occasion

This is my version of Mexican chocolate, using regular semisweet chocolate (or bittersweet chocolate plus 2 tablespoons sugar). It's cinnamony, but has more chocolate flavor than is traditional. To get the full effect of the molinillo *(page 19), the liquid must be deep enough to reach at least one of the moving rings around the main shaft, which is why this recipe is for four people. As cool as the* molinillo *looks (and sounds as it's being used), a modern wire whisk works just as well, if not better. For an even foamier drink, more like the easy version above, put the chocolate in a blender, as above, and then strain the infused milk over it; blend until the chocolate is melted.*

In a medium saucepan, heat the milk, cinnamon, vanilla bean, and salt over low heat until the milk is bubbling around the edges and almost at a simmer. Cover and set aside to steep for 5 minutes, then fish out and discard the cinnamon and vanilla bean. Add the chocolate and place over very low heat. Whisk, using a balloon whisk or a traditional wood *molinillo* (twist the *molinillo* back and forth with the handle between your palms), until the chocolate is melted and the mixture is foamy and light. Pour into 4 warmed mugs and serve immediately.

ALMOND HOT COCOA

Serves 2

½ cup pure unsweetened
   cocoa powder

¼ cup sugar

   Pinch of salt

4 teaspoons plain marzipan

1½ cups whole milk

I've found that the best way to achieve an almond flavor that is neither overpowered by the chocolate (as it is if you use plain ground almonds) nor fake-tasting and thin (as it is if you use almond extract) is to use marzipan. This cocoa is a bit sweeter than most of the others in this book—the almond flavor seems to bloom with the addition of a touch more sugar than I usually prefer.

In a 2-quart nonstick saucepan, whisk together the cocoa powder, sugar, salt, and ½ cup water until smooth. Break the marzipan into tiny pieces and add it to the pan. Cook over very low heat, whisking frequently, until the marzipan is dissolved; simmer for 2 minutes.

Pour in the milk and cook over low heat, whisking constantly, until the mixture is almost boiling; pour into 2 warmed mugs and serve immediately. If you'd like a foamier drink, blend with a handheld electric milk frother for 20 seconds just before serving.

BASIL-MINT HOT CHOCOLATE

Serves 2

1½ cups whole milk

½ cup heavy cream

½ cup fresh basil sprigs

½ cup fresh mint sprigs, plus more for garnish

Pinch of salt

2 ounces semisweet chocolate, chopped; or 2 ounces bittersweet chocolate plus 2½ teaspoons superfine sugar

It might seem odd to use a savory herb in a hot chocolate drink, but the flavor of basil is lovely with dark chocolate. Here the basil is tempered a bit by fresh mint—and by a touch more sweetness than I usually like in plain hot chocolate.

The directions may sound complicated, but this method keeps the number of pans and bowls to a minimum: Just melt the chocolate over the heating milk mixture as you would over hot water in a double boiler. If you're doubling or tripling the recipe, however, it might be more practical to melt the chocolate over a separate pan of simmering water or in a microwave oven and then combine it with the infused milk in another large bowl or saucepan.

In a 2-quart nonstick saucepan, combine the milk, cream, basil, mint, and salt. Place over very low heat. Place the chocolate in a medium heatproof bowl that fits over the top of the pan and is large enough to hold the milk mixture; set the bowl over the pan while the milk mixture is heating—double-boiler style—and melt the chocolate, stirring it frequently. Remove the pan and bowl from the heat as soon as the milk mixture begins to simmer. Let the milk mixture steep in the pan, covered by the bowl, while continuing to stir the chocolate until it's completely melted, about 2 minutes. Remove the bowl from the pan. Pour the milk mixture though a sieve into the bowl and whisk to completely incorporate the chocolate. Pour into 2 warmed mugs, garnish each with a mint sprig, and serve immediately.

CACAO NIB MASA DRINK

Serves 2 to 4

½ cup cacao nibs (see Notes)

½ cup *masa harina* (see Notes)

2½ cups whole milk

¼ to ⅓ cup honey, to taste

½ teaspoon ground cinnamon, or ¼ teaspoon ground anise

Pinch of salt

½ teaspoon pure vanilla extract

2 to 4 cinnamon sticks

This drink is an adaptation of the many recipes I've come across for Aztec and Mayan hot chocolate drinks thickened with masa. *The key is to grind your own cacao nibs instead of using regular cocoa powder. Cacao nibs, when ground, have a fresh and unusual flavor, and the little bits of nib in the drink give it a nutty texture. If you can't find nibs, substitute ⅓ cup pure unsweetened cocoa powder plus 3 tablespoons finely ground blanched almonds. You can use a* molinillo *(see page 19), if you have one, to whisk the drink to a thick froth.*

Using a coffee grinder or spice mill, grind the cacao nibs as finely as possible—this will take about 30 seconds in a standard electric spice mill. In a medium bowl, combine the cacao nibs with the masa harina. Add 1 cup of the milk and whisk to combine. Set aside.

In a 2-quart nonstick saucepan, combine the remaining 1½ cups milk with the honey, ground cinnamon, and salt. Place over medium-low heat and bring just to a boil, whisking to dissolve the honey. Immediately whisk in the masa mixture. Bring to a boil, then lower the heat and simmer, whisking frequently, for about 5 minutes, until the porridge is thick enough to hold very soft peaks when the whisk is lifted out of it. Stir in the vanilla and remove from the heat. Pour into 2 to 4 warmed cups or small bowls and insert a cinnamon stick into each one to use as a spoon for the thick drink. Serve immediately.

Notes: Cacao nibs are pieces of roasted shelled cacao beans; they can be found in specialty food stores. Masa harina, *the ground dried lime-treated corn used to make tortillas and tamales, is widely available in regular grocery stores: Look in the Hispanic foods section of the store or in the baking aisle with the other flours. Don't substitute cornmeal, as the flavor and texture are completely different.*

TASTY TEAS

Making the Perfect Pot of Tea

On chilly afternoons as the light is fading and work is becoming tedious, a pot of well-brewed Lapsang Souchong is often the only thing standing between me and a nap. It sometimes seems that the very process of making tea—paying too-close attention to the teakettle, carefully noting the tea's changing hue as it steeps, prewarming the cup and setting out the sugar and spoon, perhaps slicing a lemon—helps me to refocus when it's time to return to work.

Ingredients

Tea Leaves: For the best pot of tea, use loose tea leaves rather than tea bags, and make sure the tea is fresh: Keep small amounts of tea—ideally only enough as you can use in a few months—in opaque airtight tins or sealable canisters in a cool spot. You'll have to experiment to find the optimum amount of tea leaves to use per cup of tea—it will vary depending on the type of tea (and there are hundreds), the kind of pot you're using, and the strength of tea you prefer. A good starting point is 1 teaspoon loose tea per 6-ounce serving of black tea, less for Chinese green tea, and more for Japanese green tea.

Water: As when making coffee, the water for tea should start out cold and freshly drawn from the tap: Filter it only if your tap water isn't palatable on its own, and don't use distilled water, which tastes flat. Different varieties of tea benefit from steeping in different temperatures of water: Oolong teas, for example, are best steeped in water that hasn't come to a boil and is about 195°F. Green teas should be steeped in water that's about 180°F. Black teas generally taste best steeped in water that has come to

Page 50
Basic Chai Tea

a boil and has cooled just for a few seconds, about 210°F. The old rule of thumb—for green teas bring the kettle to the pot; for black teas bring the pot to the kettle—makes sense, but if you choose a special or expensive tea I'd suggest that you ask someone at a tea shop how to brew it, at what temperature and for how long, or consult a good book on tea, such as *The Tea Companion*, by Jane Pettigrew (Running Press 2004).

Sweetener and Other Additions: Sugar cubes, plain granulated sugar, raw sugar, honey—just a hint of sweetness, from whatever source, can bring out a tea's flavor. Experiment and use as much or as little sweetener as you like, or none at all. To English-style teas, many people add milk (never cream; and for goodness' sake never put the milk in the cup before the tea) or a slice of lemon (a slice—not a wedge, lest you be exposed as a hopeless ingrate), but never both (the acid in the lemon will curdle the milk).

TECHNIQUE

English: Put a teakettle of cold water on to boil. Meanwhile, warm up a china or ceramic teapot (see page 13) by filling it with hot tap water. When the water is boiling (don't let it boil for more than 30 seconds), empty the teapot and spoon in 1 rounded teaspoon loose tea leaves per 6-ounce serving. Pour the water over the leaves and put the lid on the pot. Let the tea steep for 3 to 5 minutes, then pour the tea through a fine-mesh strainer into individual teacups, adding sugar or honey to taste, if desired. If you don't plan to serve all the tea immediately, consider using both a brewing pot and a serving pot: Steep the tea in the first teapot, then strain it into a second warmed teapot for serving.

Alternatively, put the tea leaves in a large mesh tea ball and put it in the pot when you add the boiling water, then remove the tea ball after 3 to 5 minutes and pour the tea directly into the cups. If your teapot has a filter insert, put the tea leaves in the insert, pour water over them into the pot, cover, and let steep for 3 to 5 minutes; remove the filter insert and discard the tea leaves; then pour the tea directly into the cups.

Chinese: Chinese teas can be brewed in English teapots using the method above, or they can be steeped in a Chinese unglazed clay teapot (see page 16). The traditional Chinese tea ceremony is a complicated affair. The procedure varies from person to person, but a simplified version might play out as follows: Water is heated and used to rinse a well-seasoned clay teapot inside and out and to rinse the green tea leaves in a large bowl—the tea is placed in the pot and the water added and allowed to overflow the pot and into the bowl. Two sets of cups (one set of larger glazed cups for sniffing, one set of three-sip-capacity clay cups for drinking) are also rinsed and warmed with the first steeping of green tea. The leaves are infused a second time, for just 30 seconds or so, and the tea is poured into the cups all at once (the server should set the cups in a row so that they touch each other and pass the pot back and forth over the row to fill them). Two or more infusions of the same tea leaves follow, and the steeping time is increased by about 10 seconds each time so that, ideally, the last cup of tea tastes exactly the same as the first. Sometimes the brewed tea is poured from the teapot into a separate serving pitcher before being poured into the drinking cups. See *The Way of Tea: The Sublime Art of Oriental Tea Drinking*, by Master LAM Kam Chuen (Barron's Educational Series 2002) for a complete account of the various steps of the Chinese tea ceremony.

A selection of teapots. Clockwise from top right: a contemporary teapot with stainless-steel tea cozy, English-style ceramic pot with silver inlay, cleanly designed ceramic pot, Chinese clay pot, small teapot with cup atop, clear glass teapot with glass infuser, vintage teapot with stainless-steel tea cozy, clay teapot. Center: Japanese cast-iron tetsubin.

Tea Pots

Tea
strainers and infusers

Japanese: The Japanese *tetsubin* (see page 16), a cast-iron teapot, is one of the best ways to brew tea, particularly *sencha*, an everyday green tea (not to be confused with *matcha*, the powdered tea used in the Japanese tea ceremony). Most modern makers of *tetsubin* do not recommend using the pot on the stovetop, instead suggesting that it be treated simply as a brewing and serving teapot and that water be heated in a separate teakettle. However, if used correctly, a well-made cast-iron *tetsubin* teapot can function as an all-in-one heating, brewing, and serving container. Fill it with water and place it over a very low gas flame until the water is just simmering, then remove the pot from the heat. Insert the infuser basket, filled about halfway with tea leaves, into the water and put the lid on the pot. Let the tea steep for 2 to 3 minutes. When the tea is ready, carefully remove the insert and tea leaves and replace the lid. Pour into individual cups to serve.

Clockwise from top right: bamboo strainer, stainless-steel tea ball, paper tea bag, mesh tea ball, heart-shaped tea ball, hinged spoon-shaped tea ball, cloth tea bag, mesh tea ball, tea strainer.

BASIC CHAI TEA

Serves 2

1   cinnamon stick
6   whole allspice berries
6   whole white or green
    cardamom pods
¼   teaspoon whole black
    peppercorns
⅛   teaspoon whole fennel
    seeds
¼   teaspoon ground ginger
    Pinch of ground cloves
2   rounded teaspoons black
    Assam tea leaves
2   teaspoons sugar, or
    more to taste
1   cup whole milk

If you've only ever tried chai tea at the local coffee shop (or the redundant "chai tea latte" hawked by a certain mega-chain coffee franchise), this powerfully spicy, not-too-sweet version may come as a welcome surprise.

With the side of a cleaver or chef's knife, gently crush the whole spices, then place them in a small saucepan, along with the ground ginger, cloves, tea leaves, and sugar. Pour in 1 cup water and bring to a boil over medium heat. Cover the pan and remove from the heat; let the tea steep for 3 minutes.

Return the pan to low heat and add the milk. Bring just to a simmer, then pour through a fine-mesh sieve into 2 warmed teacups or small mugs. Serve immediately.

GREEN TEA "CAPPUCCINO"

Serves 1

1½ teaspoons green tea leaves
1 cup whole milk
1 teaspoon honey

If you'd like to double or triple this recipe, strain the milk into a large bowl; then, instead of the manual glass frother, which can accommodate only one serving, use an electric milk frother (or process in a blender) to whip the milk for several seconds.

Combine 1¼ teaspoons of the tea leaves, the milk, and honey in a small saucepan. Bring just to a simmer, stirring to dissolve the honey; immediately cover the pan and remove from the heat. Let steep for 4 minutes.

Meanwhile, in a small mortar, use a pestle to finely grind the remaining ¼ teaspoon tea leaves to a fine powder.

Pour the infused milk through a fine-mesh sieve into a manual glass milk frother. Holding the beaker steady with a potholder, plunge very gently about 10 times, to create a not-too-stiff froth on top of the milk. Pour into a large warmed coffee cup and lightly dust with the powdered tea leaves. Serve immediately.

TOASTED-BARLEY TEA

Serves 2

½ cup preferably hulled
  barley kernels
  Honey (optional)

This is how I make the popular warming, soothing, nutty Korean barley tea. You can buy barley that's been roasted specifically to use for tea, but it's easier for me to find plain barley and toast it myself. The honey is not traditional, as far as I know, but just a touch helps to bring out the grain's flavor.

In a large dry skillet or sauté pan over medium heat, toast the barley, shaking the pan and stirring constantly, for about 6 minutes, until the barley is very fragrant and deep brown. Do not let the barley burn. Immediately transfer to a bowl. (You can store cooled toasted barley in an airtight container for about 2 months before it begins to lose its flavor.)

In a small saucepan, combine the barley with 2½ cups water and bring to a boil over high heat. Reduce the heat and simmer for 5 minutes, then pour the liquid through a fine-mesh sieve into 2 warmed mugs. Sweeten lightly with honey, if desired.

Note: If you used hulled barley, put the barley itself back in the saucepan with enough water to just cover. Simmer, covered, over medium-low heat for 8 to 10 minutes, until most of the water has been absorbed and the barley is chewy-soft. This is good as a break-fast cereal (hot or cold) with a little milk and honey.

HOLIDAY SPICED TEA

Makes enough tea for several pots

Zest of 1 orange, removed in strips with a vegetable peeler

Zest of 1 lemon, removed in strips with a vegetable peeler

2 cinnamon sticks, broken into pieces

6 ounces neutral black tea leaves such as orange pekoe

When my folks visited friends in England, they brought back a tin of Taylor and Harrogate "Christmas spiced tea," a beautifully clean and simple black tea (in bags) flavored with orange, lemon, and cinnamon. This is my replication of that blend. You can of course just throw a strip each of orange and lemon zest and a cinnamon stick in with black tea leaves as you brew each pot, but the dried zest keeps well in a tin and the spiced tea makes a nice holiday gift.

Trim as much of the white pith off the inside of the strips of orange and lemon zest as possible. Lay the zest out on a sheet pan in one layer and set in a dry place, such as a turned-off oven, until completely dry and crisp. This could take up to a day, depending on the atmospheric humidity.

Put the zest in a coffee grinder or spice mill and pulse a few times to chop coarsely, until the pieces are about the size of dry tea leaves; do the same with the cinnamon. Combine the zest and cinnamon with the tea leaves and store in an airtight tin in a cool, dry place for up to several months. Use about 1 rounded teaspoon per serving of tea.

HOT TODDY

Serves 1

1   teaspoon brown sugar
1½ ounces (3 tablespoons)
    cognac
    Hot brewed black tea
1   lemon slice studded with
    3 whole cloves

The hot toddy is an endlessly adaptable drink. Try it with honey instead of brown sugar, hot water instead of tea, or even spice-infused rum instead of cognac.

Put the brown sugar and cognac in a 6- to 8-ounce Irish coffee glass or mug and stir to partially dissolve the sugar. Fill the mug with the tea, stirring to combine. Garnish with the clove-studded lemon slice. Serve immediately.

LYCHEE BLACK TEA WITH CHERRY WINE

Serves 1

3   ounces (6 tablespoons)
    cherry wine
    Hot brewed lychee
    black tea

Cherry wine or kijafa *(it's Danish) is one of those odd-looking bottles gathering dust in the corner of the local liquor store. It's sweet, and a little syrupy when cold, but I like it in mulled wines and hot drinks like this one. Lychee black tea is just tea flavored with lychee fruit, and is widely available in Chinese grocery stores. If you can't find it, substitute regular black tea plus a couple teaspoons of lychee juice such as that produced by Ceres and sold in boxes; use only 1½ ounces cherry wine to compensate for the sweetness of the lychee juice.*

Pour the wine into a warmed teacup or mug and fill the cup with the tea. Serve immediately.

SAKE AND PEAR OOLONG TEA

Serves 2

1   cup pear juice
3   teaspoons oolong
    tea leaves
¾   cup unfiltered
    Nigori sake

Combining sake with tea and fruit juices (usually citrus) isn't a new idea, but for some reason I rarely see it on drinks menus, even in fancy cocktail bars here in Manhattan. I like to use a fairly cheap unfiltered sake for this drink: The sake warms while the acidity of the tea and juice refreshes.

In a small saucepan, combine the juice and tea leaves. Place over low heat and bring to a boil. Remove from the heat and cover the pan; let steep for 3 minutes. Add the sake and bring to just below a simmer—do not boil. Strain into 2 warmed teacups or heat-proof glasses and serve immediately.

HONEYED TISANE

2   tablespoons clover or
     fancy white honey, plus
     more for serving

¾   cup packed fresh
     spearmint leaves, or 2
     tablespoons dried

½   cup packed fresh lemon
     verbena leaves, or 1
     tablespoon dried

¼   cup packed fresh
     mountain mint leaves, or
     1 tablespoon dried

1   sprig fresh basil
     Candied Lavender
     Blossoms (optional;
     page 70)

These directions are for brewing in a teapot, but of course you can simply heat 4 cups of water in a saucepan, add all the ingredients, cover the pan, and let the infusion steep. Strain the infusion into a warmed teapot or carafe for serving.

Feel free to play with the herb combination. I came up with this one when my folks lived in Virginia, where they had an extensive collection of herbs growing just outside the kitchen door and it was easy to just throw any old herbs in a pot. If you have dried herbs from your garden, you can use those instead of fresh—just cut the quantities as indicated in the recipe, and be sure to use a very fine strainer when serving.

Fill a teakettle with water and bring it to a boil over high heat.

Meanwhile, place the honey and all the herbs in a warmed 4- to 6-cup teapot. Pour enough water into the teapot to cover the herbs, pushing them down under the water with a spoon and stirring to dissolve the honey. Let steep, covered, for 4 minutes. Serve straight from the pot, pouring through a fine strainer if your teapot isn't equipped with one, with the Candied Lavender Blossoms and more honey on the side, if desired. You can add more boiling water to the herbs as the infusion is being consumed, up to a few cups more.

CANDIED LAVENDER BLOSSOMS

Makes 12

12 nice sprigs untreated lavender, with blossoms and long stems
1 large egg white
¼ cup superfine sugar

Gently rinse the lavender, shake off the excess water, and set aside on paper towels for a couple hours, until they are completely dry.

In a small bowl, beat the egg white until it's foamy and white but not stiff at all. Use a small clean paintbrush to coat a lavender sprig all over with the egg white, making sure to coat every nook and cranny of the blossoms. Sprinkle the sprig evenly all over with the superfine sugar, then stick the stem in a large block of Styrofoam to hold it upright while it dries. Repeat with the remaining lavender. Let the sprigs stand in a cool, dry spot for at least 2 hours, until completely dry. Store at room temperature in an airtight container; the candied lavender will keep for several weeks.

PERSIMMON, BLACK PEPPERCORN & GINGER TEA

Serves 2 or 3

1   medium-ripe Fuyu
     persimmon
2   ¼-inch slices fresh ginger
1   teaspoon whole black
     peppercorns
1 to 2 teaspoons sugar,
     to taste
1   rounded teaspoon green
     tea leaves (optional)
½   teaspoon pine nuts
     (optional)

This mild Korean-inspired infusion is also nice with sliced pear instead of persimmon.

Very thinly slice the persimmon horizontally, and set 2 or 3 nice slices aside for garnish. Put the remaining slices in a small saucepan with 3 cups of water, the ginger, peppercorns, and sugar. Bring to a boil, then lower the heat and simmer for 10 minutes. If using the tea, stir it in, cover the pot, and let steep off the heat for about 3 minutes. Pour through a fine-mesh sieve into small, wide, warmed cups and put a slice of fresh persimmon and a few pine nuts, if desired, in each cup. Serve immediately.

PERSIMMON TEACAKE

Serves 6 to 8

½ cup very smooth pureed persimmons (see Note)

1 large egg

½ cup whole milk

2 cups all-purpose flour

½ cup sugar

1 tablespoon baking powder

½ teaspoon salt

4 tablespoons (½ stick) unsalted butter, melted and cooled

¼ cup confectioners' sugar (optional)

Not too sweet, and very moist, this delicately flavored cake—more like a sweet bread—is perfect with a pot of tea in the afternoon.

Preheat the oven to 375°F. Butter and flour a 9-inch square cake pan (if using a silicone pan, there's no need to butter or flour it).

In a medium bowl, whisk together the persimmon puree, egg, and milk.

Into a separate large bowl, sift the flour, sugar, baking powder, and salt. Fold in the persimmon mixture until just combined, then stir in the butter. Scrape the batter into the prepared pan and smooth the top. Bake for about 15 minutes, until nicely browned on top and a toothpick inserted in the center comes out clean. Let cool for 30 minutes on a wire rack, then turn the cake out of the pan, turn it right side up, and let it cool completely on the rack. (The cake will keep at room temperature, wrapped in plastic, for several days; it can be wrapped and frozen for about 1 month.) Sift the confectioners' sugar over the top, if desired, then cut it into squares and serve.

Note: It is essential that the puree be smooth, or the cake will fall after it's baked. Pass 2 to 4 quartered ripe Fuyu persimmons through a food mill using the disk with the finest holes; or peel and then blend the persimmons in a blender, then push them through a fine-mesh sieve. Discard the peels and any stringy fibers.

CINNAMON-CHILE INFUSION WITH DRIED JUJUBES

Serves 2 or 3

3 sticks good-quality cinnamon
2 ¼-inch slices fresh ginger
1 small dried hot chile, such as arbol
4 dried jujubes ("Chinese dates"), halved and pitted, 1 minced, for garnish, if desired
½ teaspoon sugar, or to taste (optional)

One of my favorite spices is cinnamon, and this infusion is about as purely cinnamony as anything I've ever made. The fiery heat of chile and ginger, combined with the dense sweetness of dried jujubes, makes for a warming, invigorating drink.

Dried jujubes, sometimes labeled "red Chinese dates," can be found in foil-lined pouches hanging in Chinese grocery stores. They taste like a cross between dates and raisins—dates would make a fine (though more expensive) substitute here.

Put the cinnamon, ginger, chile, the halved jujubes, and the sugar, if using, in a small saucepan with 2½ cups of water. Bring to a boil, then lower the heat and simmer for 10 minutes, or until the infusion is very fragrant and a deep caramel color. Pour through a fine-mesh sieve into small warmed cups and add a bit of the minced jujube to each serving, if using. Serve immediately.

COZY COFFEE DRINKS

Making the Perfect Cup of Coffee

I drink a lot of coffee—morning, noon, and night. Usually I need a pot of regular drip coffee to get me through the morning. But I appreciate—indeed, require—variety in most things, and making different styles of coffee, and using different types of beans, is the best way to keep the stuff interesting. So in the afternoon, or in the evening before going out to meet friends who might wish to engage in a level of conversation (semi-intelligent) to which only caffeine can elevate me, I'll make a batch of coffee in the French press, or pull a shot of espresso. If the night promises to be a long one, I might even prescribe myself a cup of Melya (page 104).

Ingredients

Coffee Beans: This isn't the place to go into all the different varieties of coffee available—from Colombian Arabica to Jamaican Blue Mountain. Use whatever kind you prefer. In the coffee recipes here, I used a standard whole-bean French roast, usually ground relatively fine, 25 seconds in a regular rotary-blade coffee or spice mill, or at the 6 or 7 near-espresso-fine setting in a burr grinder (see pages 11 and 12), and brewed it in a good electric drip machine to produce a dark, strong coffee perfect for mixing with other ingredients. Sometimes I used a French press to make the coffee, and used a much coarser grind. The important thing is that the coffee is strong, bold enough to stand up to, say, a shot of brandy and one of crème de cacao. In the espresso recipes, I used, naturally, whole-bean Italian espresso and ground it as fine as possible in the burr grinder. (This required a fair amount of expletive-studded recalibration efforts on my part, but was worth the effort.)

Page 76:
Koreatown Cuban Coffee
with hot buttered roll.

Keep coffee beans or ground coffee in an airtight, opaque container in a cool spot, and grind in small batches if possible. It's not necessary to refrigerate coffee unless it isn't going to be used within a week or so.

Water: If your tap water is good enough to drink on its own, it's good enough for making coffee. Whether you filter it or not, start with cold water that's freshly drawn from the tap rather than water that's been sitting in the filter pitcher in the fridge or on the counter all day. Cold, fresh water has more oxygen in it, which supposedly improves the flavor of the coffee (although my coarse palate doesn't seem to be sensitive enough to tell the difference in drip-brewed coffee made with stale versus fresh water). Don't use distilled water, which is lacking the flavorful minerals found in tap water.

TECHNIQUE

Manual Drip: The manual drip method is the simplest and, many experts claim, the best way to make coffee. Put about 2 scant tablespoons ground coffee (a standard coffee measuring scoop holds a little less than 1 tablespoon) per 8-ounce cup in the filter in the filter holder on top of the manual drip pot (see page 9), pour in a little hot water (just off the boil) to cover the grounds and allow them to bloom, then a few seconds later pour in more water, until the desired amount of coffee has dripped through the filter into the pot. Until companies start manufacturing transparent thermal carafes, be sure you measure the water before you boil it in the teakettle so you know you're pouring in the right amount. Or use a clear coffee pot and drink the coffee quickly, before it gets cold.

Electric Drip: Electric drip coffee makers (see page 9) are by far the most common in the United States, and operate on the same principle as manual drip coffee pots: Hot water is passed through coffee grounds, by the force of gravity, into a pot. Again, use 2 scant tablespoons per cup of coffee. Follow the instructions that came with your coffee maker to brew the coffee. If it has a burner to keep the coffee warm rather than a thermal carafe, try to limit the coffee's time on the heat to 30 minutes, or it will turn bitter.

Neapolitan Drip: If you can get a good Neapolitan pot (see page 9), and not one of the cheap new ones that isn't worth its weight as scrap metal, it's a great way to make small batches of coffee on the stovetop. Fill the bottom half of the pot with cold water to just below the tiny steam-release hole in the side of the pot, put the filter on top and fill it about three-quarters full with medium-ground coffee, then put the top section of the pot over the filter. Place the pot over high heat to bring the water in the bottom to a boil (it'll sputter out the hole when it's boiling), then hold both the top and bottom handles and flip the whole contraption over so that the water filters down through the coffee and into the empty pot—the one with a pouring spout. If you've got a good model, you won't end up with coffee spurting out all over your kitchen.

Vietnamese Drip: This is another somewhat imperfect way of making drip coffee, but it does produce a fine after-meal beverage. (You might want to begin the process of making your cup of coffee when you're about halfway through your bowl of pho, or at least distract yourself with some other amusement—a *Simpsons* episode or two?—while it's dripping, because this method takes a lifetime to produce actual coffee.) Vietnamese filters (see page 10) are individual coffee makers, so if you're having friends over for spring rolls and noodle soup, you'll need one filter set for each person. Vietnamese coffee is almost always heavily sweetened: In each empty coffee cup, put about 2 tablespoons sweetened condensed milk. A small glass is best—4- to 6-ounce capacity: Make sure its rim is narrow enough to fit inside the filter's ring holder. Bring a teakettle of water to a boil. Meanwhile, unscrew the perforated inner disk and remove it from the outer cup. Place 2 tablespoons medium-ground coffee into the cup and replace the disk, screwing it on just until it's snug against the coffee but not tight. Place the filter's ring on top of the coffee cup and nestle the filter cup in the ring. Pour in enough hot water (just off the boil) to come about halfway to the top of the screw on the perforated disk; wait a few seconds, then loosen the disk slightly to allow for expansion of the wet coffee grounds. Put the lid on top to retain at least some of the heat (the lids never fit quite right), and keep adding water to the filter cup until you've brewed 3 or 4 ounces—this will take a long time. When the coffee is done, remove the lid and flip it over on the table; lift the filter cup off the coffee cup and set it on the overturned lid; remove the ring from the coffee cup. Either stir up the condensed milk from the bottom of the cup or consider it the dessert at the end of a lengthy meal of good, dense, at best lukewarm coffee. (Vietnamese coffee is also often served iced: Just put the condensed milk in a tall glass, fill the glass with ice, and brew hot coffee over it; stir it all up when the coffee's done brewing.)

French Press: Now that—finally—insulated French-press coffee makers (see page 10) are more widely available, and now that some of them feature a nifty swiveling disk that allows you to cut off the extraction of the grounds at the correct time, and now that they also have fine-mesh strainers in the spout to catch stray grounds, I have no more excuses not to brew coffee using this method. Put a teakettle of water on to boil. Put 2 tablespoons coarse-ground coffee per 8-ounce serving in the bottom of the French press. Pour in hot water (just off the boil), stir, then put the lid on (with the plunger screen in the up position) and let the coffee steep for about 4 minutes. Press the plunger screen down until it stops; if your French press has a disk to close off the screen and keep the coffee from further contact with the grounds, turn the handle to close it.

Turkish Ibrik: Turkish coffee is extremely strong and so thick that you aren't even expected to drink the last quarter or third of the coffee in your cup—all the sludge settles to the bottom and is quite unpalatable to say the least. The stuff is made in an *ibrik* (see page 10), a small stove-top pot that bulges out a bit at the bottom, cinches in a bit toward the top, and then flares out at the rim, with a long handle. It definitely takes some practice, but when you get the hang of it, using an *ibrik* is a fairly effective way to make a strong cup of coffee. For Turkish coffee it's essential that you use very fine, powdered coffee; it needs to be finer than you can grind it yourself, so go ahead and buy a bag or can of pre-ground Turkish- or Greek-style coffee.

Fill the *ibrik* with cold water to about two fingers below its cinched waist, or about two thirds full, and stir in as much sugar as desired (Turkish coffee should be relatively sweet—1 teaspoon sugar per 2-ounce serving is considered normal). Sprinkle powdered Turkish or Greek coffee onto the top of the water—it will float for a while and form a seal over the water; do not stir the coffee in. It's not possible to make half a pot of Turkish coffee, so the dosing will always be the same for whatever size *ibrik* you use. A standard 3-inch-high *ibrik* will make about 4 servings: Use about 8 ounces (1 cup) water, 4 teaspoons sugar, and 4 teaspoons coffee. Place the *ibrik* over medium heat and watch it carefully—

Clockwise from left: Neopolitan flip pot, French press, milk frother, machinetta, Turkish ibrik. Center: Vietnamese drip filter.

Coffee Makers

do not take your eyes off it. As soon as the water foams up to the top of the *ibrik*, remove it from the heat and let it settle for 10 seconds. Return it to medium heat and let it foam up again (this time it will foam up almost immediately), then remove it from the heat to settle for 10 seconds. Place the *ibrik* back over medium heat and let it foam up once more, then remove from the heat and let the coffee settle for 10 seconds. Use a spoon to hold back any foam on top of the coffee as you slowly pour it into demitasse cups, leaving the sludge in the bottom of the *ibrik*. Spoon a bit of any foam over the top of each serving.

One-Pot (Camp) Coffee: Every once in a while it's instructive to make coffee the old-fashioned way, if only to experience what coffee might have tasted like a hundred years ago. This method may be more trouble than using a coffee maker (there's a reason the things were invented), but if you're making a big breakfast of fried trout and such why not use one more burner, or make space over the fire, for a pan of camp coffee?

In a saucepan or stovetop coffee pot over high heat (or over the glowing coals of a live fire, preferably near a high mountain trout stream), bring water to a boil. Pull the pan off the heat and add 1 heaping table-spoon ground coffee for every 1 cup water, then add 1 more heaping tablespoon; return the pan to low heat. Cook at a slow simmer (a bubble or two every few seconds) for 5 to 7 minutes—do not let the coffee boil (boiled coffee's spoiled coffee, you know). Let the grounds settle for 30 seconds or so, then ladle or pour the coffee into mugs—through a small fine-mesh sieve if you're picky about such things—I mean, this is camp coffee, after all.

Espresso: The simple Italian stovetop espresso maker, or *macchineta* (see page 10), allows you to make small amounts of coffee—espresso, actually—with very little fuss. Using one of these things is a darn-near-foolproof operation. Unscrew the top section and set it aside. Take the funnel-shaped filter out of the bottom section. Fill the bottom with cold water to just below the steam-release valve, the little screw on the side of the vessel. Replace the funnel filter and fill it almost to the top with finely ground espresso, smoothing the top but not tamping it or compressing it at all. With the perforated disk and gasket in place on the bottom of the top section of the *macchineta*, screw on the top section. Place the whole thing over high heat (if you're using a gas burner, the flames should cover but not extend beyond the bottom of the *macchineta*).

When the water comes to a boil, steam will rise up through the espresso grounds and come out the spout inside the top section— you'll hear it sputtering. As the sputtering sound dissipates, remove the *macchineta* from the heat and pour the espresso into demitasse cups.

A top-of-the-line pump-driven home electric espresso machine (see page 10) can come pretty close to producing café-quality shots of espresso, but using one that isn't fully automatic requires some practice. Read the manual that comes with your machine. My KitchenAid yields a very fine shot—as long as I do everything exactly right. If I cut a single corner, the espresso is noticeably the poorer for it. Following are some of the steps that you might be tempted to skip or gloss over but shouldn't:

- The coffee must be extremely finely ground (only a burr coffee grinder can achieve this, unfortunately, but you can also just use good—that is, expensive, Italian—preground espresso).

- The filter basket should be preheated by putting it into the brew-head while the boilers heat the water, and then it should be wiped off with a dry towel before the grounds are added to it.

- The coffee grounds must be dosed accurately into the portafilter's filter basket (1 tablespoon plus 1 teaspoon for a single shot, I've found, is about right).

- The grounds must be tamped firmly, so that the surface of the grounds is even and perfectly level—don't rush through this step, or the water will overextract some grounds and underextract others, which results in a thin, weak, very bitter shot.

- The water in the boiler or boilers must come to the highest possible temperature—this takes 5 to 6 minutes in my machine—before the espresso is drawn; each boiler's dial should register at the top end of the "ready" zone.

BASIC CAPPUCCINO

Serves 1

1   ounce (1 shot) espresso
4   ounces (½ cup) steamed
    or hot milk
    Foamed milk

Cappuccino, contrary to popular opinion, is not one-third espresso, one-third steamed milk, one-third foamed milk. Here are the correct proportions.

If you're using an electric espresso machine (see pages 85–86 for more information about how to use them), brew the espresso into a wide 6-ounce coffee cup. Steam the milk in a stainless-steel pitcher, using the frothing arm of the espresso machine. With a large soup spoon, hold back the foam on top of the milk as you pour enough steamed milk into the espresso to almost fill the cup, then spoon the froth on top to fill and extend above the rim of the cup. Serve immediately.

If you're using a stovetop espresso maker (see page 85), heat about ½ cup milk in a small saucepan until it's just steaming as you brew the espresso. Pour the milk into a manual glass frother (see page 16) and carefully froth the hot milk, holding the beaker steady with a potholder; alternatively, use an electric milk frother (see page 16) to froth the hot milk in the saucepan. Pour 1 ounce of espresso into a wide 6-ounce coffee cup, then pour in enough hot milk to almost fill the cup. Dollop with the foam and serve immediately.

KOREATOWN CUBAN COFFEE

Serves 1

2   teaspoons sweetened
    condensed milk or sugar,
    or to taste
1   ounce (1 shot) hot espresso
6   ounces (¾ cup) steamed
    or hot whole milk

When I had an office job on West Thirty-Fifth Street in Manhattan and was inspired by my work to take excessively long lunch breaks, I'd (too) often treat myself to Korean food followed by a stop at a little coffee hut where a Latina woman sold what she called "Cuban coffee," which was sort of like a jumpy-sweet version of café con leche. I'd usually get it iced, but hot is just as good. Have a buttered Cuban roll on the side, of course.

Put the sweetened condensed milk or sugar in an 8-ounce coffee mug or heatproof glass and pour in the espresso (or brew the espresso directly into the mug). Stir to combine thoroughly, then pour in the steamed milk and stir again. Serve immediately.

CAFÉ MOCHA WITH COFFEE WHIPPED CREAM

Serves 2

½ cup heavy cream

½ teaspoon confectioners' sugar

½ teaspoon instant espresso powder, plus more for garnish

1 cup Basic Hot Cocoa or Basic Hot Chocolate (pages 30 and 28)

1 cup hot, strong, brewed coffee

In a chilled stainless-steel bowl, combine the cream, sugar, and instant espresso powder. Whip with a chilled balloon whisk until the espresso powder is dissolved and the cream holds soft peaks. (Alternatively, place the cream, sugar, and espresso powder in a tall glass and use an electric milk frother (see page 16) to beat the mixture until the cream holds very soft peaks. The cream will be denser and smoother, and will have less volume than hand-whipped cream.)

Fill 2 warmed 6- to 8-ounce mugs or Irish coffee cups halfway with the cocoa, then add the coffee. Top with the whipped cream and dust each serving with a pinch of espresso powder.

WALNUT-CHERRY BISCOTTI

Makes about 3 dozen

1 cup cherry wine, brandy, or water

½ cup dried cherries

1 cup roughly chopped walnuts

2 cups all-purpose flour

⅔ cup sugar

½ teaspoon baking powder

¼ teaspoon salt

2 tablespoons unsalted butter

2 large eggs

2 large egg yolks

1 teaspoon pure vanilla extract

2 ounces white chocolate (optional)

Preheat the oven to 350°F. Place the wine in a small saucepan over medium heat. Bring to a boil and pour it over the cherries in a small dish; let the cherries soak for about 30 minutes. Spread the walnuts out on a baking sheet and toast in the oven for 10 minutes. Remove to a plate and let cool. Grease and lightly flour a baking sheet or line a baking sheet with parchment or a Silpat.

In a medium bowl, combine the flour, sugar, baking powder, and salt. Add the butter and pinch it with your fingers until it's in small shards and evenly distributed in the flour mixture. In a small bowl, beat together the eggs, egg yolks, and vanilla and add them to the flour mixture. Stir gently with a wooden spoon until just combined; the dough will be sticky and very soft. Transfer half of the dough to the baking sheet and shape it, using lightly floured hands, into a log about 12 inches long, 2 inches wide, and ½ inch high. Repeat with the second half of the dough. Bake for about 30 minutes, until light golden and set but still soft. Remove from the oven and lower the oven temperature to 300°F.

Transfer one biscotti log to a cutting board and very carefully, using a sharp serrated knife and holding the log steady with a towel, slice it crosswise on the diagonal into ½-inch cookies. Lay the cookies on their side on the baking sheet and repeat with the second log. Bake the cookies for 10 to 12 minutes, until light brown. Remove to a wire rack to cool and become crisp.

Finely chop the white chocolate, if using, and place it in the top of a double boiler or in a small bowl set over a pan of simmering water. When almost melted, remove it from the heat and stir until completely melted. Use a spoon to drizzle the white chocolate over the cooled biscotti. Let stand until the chocolate has set. The biscotti will keep, stored in an airtight container, for about 2 weeks.

CHICORY COFFEE

The roots of the chicory plant (Cichorium intybus; it's related to dandelion), roasted and ground, were at one time used in the South to stretch more expensive coffee, and some people developed a taste for chicory-enhanced coffee. Nowadays, premixed and ground chicory coffee can be more expensive than pure coffee—which doesn't make much sense when you can walk down just about any country road with a trowel and a basket and dig up chicory roots to roast yourself. (Consult a plant-identification book such as Stalking the Wild Asparagus, *by Euell Gibbons [Alan C. Hood & Co. 1962], if you're not sure what the chicory plant looks like.)*

Trim any leaves off the taproots (the thick root that looks like a miniature brown parsnip) and wash and scrub the roots well. Chop them into small chunks (a plant clipper will work better than a cleaver for this—those darn roots can be tough), then spread them out on a baking sheet in a warm oven—about 225°F—until they're dry all the way through; this could take 2 to 3 hours. Store the roots in an airtight tin or jar in a cool spot, and use them within a few months—after that they start to taste distinctly of dirt.

Grind the roasted roots in a food processor, coffee grinder, or heavy-duty spice mill as finely as you can (they won't become as fine as ground coffee, but get as close to that consistency as possible). Use about one part chicory to one part coffee when brewing coffee using any of the drip methods, the French press method, or the one-pot method (see pages 9–10).

Note: My mom says that you can save the larger chicory taproots and lay them out flat in a pot of damp soil, cover the pot with black plastic or a board, and set it aside in a cool dark place. The tiny, blanched yellow-white leaves that sprout from the root are good in salads.

REAL IRISH COFFEE

Serves 1

3   ounces (6 tablespoons) good Irish whiskey
5   ounces (½ cup plus 3 tablespoons) hot, strong brewed coffee
    Softly whipped heavy cream

Some bartenders sweeten their Irish coffee, either by partially dissolving a teaspoon or so of sugar (white or brown) in the whiskey before pouring in the coffee or by using sweetened whipped cream, but I don't find the added sugar to be necessary if you use a fine Irish whiskey such as Powers or Jameson. The cream should be very cold and softly whipped, just to the point that it holds droopy peaks—it should not be stiff or firm. You can whip the cream quite easily by hand, as you should stop whipping long before your arm tires anyway. Finally, by no means should anything green be drizzled on top.

Put the whiskey in a warmed 6- to 8-ounce Irish coffee glass and fill the glass with the coffee. Dollop with softly whipped cream.

HOT PENNY RUM

Serves 1

1½ ounces (3 tablespoons) rum

½ ounce (1 tablespoon) bourbon

½ ounce (1 tablespoon) crème de cacao

Hot, strong, brewed coffee

2 tablespoons cold heavy cream, very softly whipped

Hot penny rum (as far as I know, the origin of the name has been lost to history) is a classic hot drink that deserves a bit of a revival—it's potent, with a hint of chocolate from the crème de cacao, and richness from the cold whipped cream on top.

Put the rum, bourbon, and crème de cacao in a warmed 6- to 8-ounce Irish coffee glass. Fill almost to the top with the coffee. Spoon the cream onto the top of the drink and serve immediately.

COFFEE GROG

Serves 1

1 tablespoon Spiced
 Sweetened Butter
 (recipe follows)

1½ ounces (3 tablespoons)
 dark rum

¾ cup very hot, strong,
 brewed coffee

 Softly whipped heavy
 cream

 Pinch of grated
 orange zest

Makes enough for 8 drinks

8 tablespoons (1 stick)
 salted butter, softened

2 tablespoons dark
 brown sugar

½ teaspoon ground
 cinnamon

⅛ teaspoon freshly
 grated nutmeg

⅛ teaspoon ground
 cloves

¼ teaspoon grated
 orange zest

¼ teaspoon grated
 lemon zest

Grogs, like toddies, are quite adaptable—there are almost no fixed ingredients in the classic drink. Instead of rum and coffee, try brandy and hot water or tea, or even tequila and hot water, and sweeten with Cointreau instead of the spiced butter.

Put the spiced butter in a mug or Irish coffee glass and add the rum and coffee; stir to partially melt the butter. Top with the softly whipped cream and sprinkle with orange zest. Serve immediately.

Spiced Sweetened Butter

In a small bowl, combine all the ingredients, beating well with a spoon or stiff spatula to thoroughly incorporate the brown sugar and spices into the butter. Use immediately, or place the butter mixture on a sheet of wax paper or plastic wrap and roll it into a log shape about the size of the original stick of butter, twisting the paper together at the ends to smooth out the log. The butter will keep in the refrigerator for up to 2 weeks.

SWISS COFFEE COCKTAIL

Serves 1

1½ ounces (3 tablespoons) peppermint schnapps

1 ounce (2 tablespoons) crème de cacao

Hot, strong, brewed coffee

2 tablespoons or more cold heavy cream, very softly whipped

I'm incapable of getting cream to float on top of a cocktail. All that business about pouring it over the back of a spoon? It does not work—at least not for me. It is nice, though, to sip the hot drink through a layer of cold cream, so what I do is just run a whisk through the cream a few times in a small bowl before spooning it on.

Pour the schnapps, crème de cacao, and coffee into a warmed 6- to 8-ounce Irish coffee glass. Spoon the cream onto the top of the drink and serve immediately.

CAFÉ BRÛLOT WITH CINNAMON CREAM

Serves 2

½ cup heavy cream

½ teaspoon good-quality ground cinnamon, preferably Vietnamese

¾ cup brandy

6 tablespoons Cointreau

2 3-inch strips orange zest, removed with a vegetable peeler

6 whole allspice berries

1 cinnamon stick

1 cup hot, very strong, brewed coffee, preferably French-press (see page 81)

The classic café brûlot is a somewhat fancy affair, requiring either flameproof glassware or a chafing dish for igniting the liquors in front of ooh-ing and ahh-ing guests. If you're making it for two people it's easier (not to mention less ostentatious) to simply ignite the liquors in a saucepan in the kitchen, then pour everything into mugs or heatproof glasses. Don't let the flame burn too long before adding the coffee, or too much of the alcohol will burn off.

In a chilled stainless-steel bowl with a chilled balloon whisk, or using an immersion (stick) blender with the cream-whipping attachment, whip the cream together with the ground cinnamon until soft peaks form. Set aside.

In a medium saucepan, combine the brandy, Cointreau, orange zest, allspice, and cinnamon stick. Place over low heat and cook until the mixture is just hot and steaming but not boiling, about 4 minutes. Making sure there are no flammable materials nearby, remove from the heat and carefully use a lit match to ignite the liquor, then pour in the coffee. Pour through a sieve into 2 warmed mugs or Irish coffee glasses and dollop with the cinnamon whipped cream. Serve immediately.

SWEETENED ESPRESSO WITH GRAPPA

Serves 1

1   ounce (1 shot) hot espresso
1   teaspoon sugar
1½ ounces (3 tablespoons)
    grappa

When the Italian-American owner-operators of the restaurant where I worked for a time made espresso for themselves, this is how they consumed it. I've never heard of anyone else, Italian or not, drinking espresso and grappa like this. Though this may seem like a horrifyingly gauche practice, if you use one of the more interesting infused grappas (I especially liked a pine-needle grappa I tasted at a rifugio *outside Trento last spring) the drink's appeal becomes more C. K. Dexter Haven, less Mike Connor.*

In a small espresso cup, stir the sugar into the espresso until it's dissolved. Drink the espresso. Stir the grappa into the sludge and residual *crema* at the bottom and up the sides of the cup. Drink the grappa.

CRUNCHY ESPRESSO-BEAN CHOCOLATES

Makes about 2 dozen

6 ounces bittersweet chocolate

1 tablespoon salted butter

2 tablespoons whole espresso beans

Line a half-sheet pan with wax paper or a Silpat.

Finely chop the chocolate and place it and the butter in the top of a double boiler over simmering water. Cook, stirring frequently, until the chocolate is just melted. Lift the top of the double boiler from the bottom and set aside.

Crush the espresso beans gently with the flat side of a chef's knife; there should be some large pieces or even whole beans, and some smaller pieces. Stir the beans into the chocolate mixture, then spoon teaspoonfuls of the mixture onto the prepared sheet pan to form 1½-inch medallions. Chill in the refrigerator until firm, then peel the chocolates off the wax paper or Silpat. The chocolates will keep in the refrigerator, in a resealable plastic bag, for at least 1 week.

MELYA

Serves 1

1   teaspoon pure
    unsweetened cocoa
    powder
    About 1 teaspoon honey
1   ounce (1 shot) espresso

Melya is some crazy stuff, let me tell you. At around ten thirty on this most recent New Year's Eve, as my fella and I stirred and stirred and stirred two cups of honey and cocoa powder with fussy miniature spoons, I had the distinct feeling that we were engaging in some sort of drug-related ritual. And about ten minutes after downing my cup of melya I knew that's exactly what we'd been doing. Melya's a sugar high, a chocolate high, and a coffee high in one concentrated dose.

In a demitasse cup, stir the cocoa powder and honey together until smooth and gooey—this will take at least 1 minute: Keep stirring until it's shiny and smooth. Pour in the espresso (or, better, brew it directly into the cup) and stir well to combine. Serve immediately.

DRINKS TO WARM BODY & SOUL

Having a pan of mulled cider or wine on the stovetop is a fine excuse to throw a holiday party—or to just call some friends over to share the warmth on a cold winter's night. The drinks in this chapter, many of them alcohol based, are best when made in larger batches. Following are a few tips for serving hot drinks without fuss.

THE MESS

There's no good way to transfer a hot drink—especially hot chocolates or cocoas—directly from saucepan to mug without half of it puddling up around the bottom of the mug and the other half on the kitchen floor. The straight-pour method? Disaster. The ladle method? Ineffective. The overdesigned-ladle-with-a-convenient-looking-pour-spout-and-ergonomic-handle method? Expensively ineffective. If you're not putting the drink in a carafe or an urn to pour out during a party, your only hope is a large glass measuring cup: As you're preparing the drink, measure the liquids into a large glass liquid measuring cup (a heatproof one with a spout and clear markings, such as those made by Pyrex); when the drink is ready to be served, quickly and carefully pour it from the saucepan back into the measuring cup—through a strainer or sieve, if necessary—then pour from the measuring cup into the mugs.

COFFEE FOR A CROWD

Simply make several pots of coffee in a regular automatic drip machine, and transfer the coffee to a stainless-steel urn; light a can of Sterno underneath the urn (an urn with an adjustable Sterno holder will ensure that you don't over- or underheat the coffee—taste the coffee from time to time to make sure it's the

Page 106:
Glügg

right temperature). For Coffee Grog (page 96), tell your guests to put a shot of rum in their mug, along with a spoonful or slice of Spiced Sweetened Butter (page 96), and then fill the mug with coffee from the urn. An air-pump thermal-insulated coffee dispenser—like the one they use at coffee shops—is another good way to serve coffee at parties.

FLAMING PRESENTATION

For a flashy, party-worthy presentation of Café Brûlot (page 100), double or triple the quantities in the recipe. Warm the liquors, orange zest, and spices in a large saucepan, then carefully pour them into a small (3 1/2 quart) stainless-steel chafing dish and light a Sterno can underneath. Have the hot coffee ready in a carafe or coffee pot. Use a long match to ignite the warmed liquors, then pour in the coffee to douse the flame. Serve with a ladle, leaving the orange zest and spices in the chafing dish.

SLOW-COOKER SERVICE

One of the easiest, most convenient ways to serve large quantities of hot drinks for parties is to make them in a slow cooker (or Crock Pot). It's especially appropriate for Glügg or Mulled Wine (pages 110 and 111). Put all the ingredients in a $3^{1}/_{2}$- or 4-quart slow cooker (double the recipe for Mulled Wine and put the Glügg spices in a cheesecloth bag) and cook, covered, on the high or low setting until well heated and just beginning to bubble at the edges, 1 to 2 hours. When you're ready to serve the drink, uncover the cooker, remove and discard the spice bag, and ladle the drink into heatproof glasses or mugs. Turn the heat setting to warm or low to keep the wine warm throughout the party.

GLÜGG

Serves 8 to 10

2 750-milliliter bottles dry red wine

Zest of 1 orange, removed in strips with a vegetable peeler

2 tablespoons whole white or green cardamom pods

1 tablespoon whole cloves

2 cinnamon sticks

1 2-inch piece fresh ginger, halved

1 cup sugar

1 cup golden raisins

2 cups aquavit (caraway-flavored Swedish liquor)

1 cup blanched whole almonds

Any full-bodied red wine will work well in glügg and other mulled wines—I like the less-expensive New World Cabernets, the drier the better.

The day before you plan to serve the glügg (or early in the morning), pour the wine into a nonreactive pitcher and add the orange zest, cardamom, cloves, cinnamon, and ginger. Let stand at room temperature for at least 12 hours, then strain the wine into a large saucepan or pot and discard the spices.

Add the sugar and raisins and place the pan over medium-low heat, stirring until the sugar is dissolved; do not allow the wine to boil. Add the aquavit and almonds and bring back to just below a boil. Ladle the glügg along with some raisins and almonds into heat-proof glasses. Serve each glass with a spoon for the fruit and nuts.

MULLED WINE

Serves 4 to 6

Zest of 1 large orange, removed in strips with a vegetable peeler, 4 to 6 long twists reserved for garnish

Zest of 1 lemon, removed in strips with a vegetable peeler

4   cinnamon sticks, plus 4 to 6 more for garnish

1   rounded tablespoon whole allspice berries

1   rounded tablespoon whole cloves

6   whole black peppercorns (optional)

1   750-milliliter bottle dry, full-bodied red wine

⅓ to ½ cup brown sugar, to taste

1   cup brandy

¼   cup Cointreau or other orange liqueur (optional)

I like the spiciness of just a few peppercorns in the mulled wine spice mix, but feel free to omit them for a more traditional flavor. For a thoughtful gift to party hosts, make a big batch of the spices and tie up several bags—or put the mulling spices in pretty tins.

Tie the orange and lemon zest strips, 4 cinnamon sticks, the allspice, cloves, and peppercorns, if using, in a cheesecloth bag and place in a large saucepan or pot. Add the wine and brown sugar and place over medium heat. Bring just to a boil, then immediately lower the heat and simmer for 10 minutes, stirring to dissolve the brown sugar. Add the brandy and Cointreau, if using, and cook until just heated through but not boiling. Taste for sweetness, and add more brown sugar if necessary. Remove and discard the spice bag and pour the mulled wine into a carafe, or ladle into heatproof glasses. Garnish each serving with a cinnamon stick and orange twist.

MULLED WHITE WINE WITH PEACH JUICE

Serves 2

1½ cups dry or semidry
    white wine, such as
    Sauvignon Blanc

½ cup peach juice

2   lemon slices

1   ¼-inch slice fresh ginger,
    or ⅛ teaspoon ground
    ginger

⅛ teaspoon ground
    cinnamon

2   teaspoons honey

2   large slices crystallized
    ginger for garnish

This was inspired by a peach and ginger pie I made once, for a book club meeting (Dogeaters, as I recall, but nobody had read the book). I never thought this could be true, but the drink may be better than the pie.

Combine all the ingredients except the crystallized ginger in a small saucepan and place over the lowest possible heat. Stir to dissolve the honey. Bring just to a simmer and cook for 2 minutes; do not let the wine come to a boil. Discard the lemon slices and fresh ginger slice and pour the wine into 2 warmed mugs or heatproof glasses; garnish the rims of the mugs or glasses with the crystallized ginger and serve immediately.

HOT BUTTERED BOURBON

Serves 2

1½ cups apple cider, or 1½
    cups water plus 2 table-
    spoons brown sugar

2   cinnamon sticks

1   rounded teaspoon whole
    allspice berries

½   rounded teaspoon
    whole cloves

¼   teaspoon ground ginger

¾   cup bourbon

2   slices Nutmeg Butter

*Makes enough for about
16 drinks*

8   tablespoons (1 stick)
    salted butter, at room
    temperature

¼   teaspoon freshly grated
    nutmeg

½   teaspoon confectioners'
    sugar

*Hot buttered bourbon is usually made with plain water, and
sweetened, but I like to use cider instead. This is also excellent
with rum or brandy instead of bourbon.*

In a small saucepan, combine the cider, cinnamon, allspice,
cloves, and ginger and place over low heat. Cook at a simmer
for 5 minutes. Stir in the bourbon and bring back to a simmer;
immediately remove from the heat. Pour into 2 warmed mugs
and top each with a slice of Nutmeg Butter.

Nutmeg Butter

Put all the ingredients in a small bowl and stir with a rubber spatula
to combine. Place the butter mixture on a sheet of wax paper or
plastic wrap and roll it into a log shape about the size of the original
stick of butter, twisting the paper together at the ends to smooth
out the log. Chill in the freezer for about 30 minutes, until firm but
not frozen hard. Slice into ¼-inch (½-tablespoon) rounds to use in
buttered drinks. The butter will keep, frozen and tightly wrapped,
for at least a month; let it stand at room temperature for 30 minutes
before slicing it. It'll keep in the refrigerator for about 2 weeks.

*Note: To double the recipe, after heating the cider, transfer it (with
or without the spices) to a prewarmed thermal carafe (a 34-ounce
carafe will work). When serving each guest, pour about a shot and a
half of bourbon into a mug, fill it with the cider, and top with the
Nutmeg Butter.*

SPICED CANDIED NUTS

Makes 5 cups

4   tablespoons (½ stick) butter, melted, plus more for the pans
2   large egg whites
¾   teaspoon salt
½   cup sugar
1   teaspoon Hungarian paprika
1   teaspoon ground cumin
½   teaspoon ground cayenne
½   teaspoon granulated garlic (or garlic powder)
2   cups walnut halves
2   cups pecan halves
1   cup roasted cashews

Preheat the oven to 350°F. Butter 2 quarter-sheet pans or a large rimmed baking sheet, preferably nonstick.

In a large bowl, using a whisk or an electric beater, beat the egg whites together with the salt until foamy, white, and about tripled in volume. Gradually beat in the sugar, then the paprika, cumin, cayenne, and granulated garlic.

Add the nuts, and pour in the butter. Stir with a spatula until the nuts are evenly coated with the egg-white mixture, then spread the nuts out in one layer on the prepared sheet pans. Bake, stirring occasionally, for 25 to 30 minutes, until the nuts are well browned. Transfer the nuts to a clean pan and let them cool to room temperature; the nuts will become crisp as they cool. Store in an airtight container at room temperature for up to 1 week.

CLASSIC MULLED CIDER

Serves 4

4 cups apple cider

¾ cup brown sugar, or to taste

Zest of 1 large orange, removed in strips with a vegetable peeler

2 rounded tablespoons whole cloves

1 rounded tablespoon whole allspice berries

2 teaspoons ground cinnamon

½ teaspoon ground ginger

¼ teaspoon freshly grated nutmeg

4 cinnamon sticks for garnish

I'll admit I like my mulled cider sweet and strong. That means plenty of brown sugar (cider seems to become much less sweet after it's been heated—I've no idea why), and abundant spices, especially numbing cloves.

Combine all the ingredients except the cinnamon sticks in a medium saucepan over medium heat and bring to a boil, whisking to incorporate the cinnamon and ginger and dissolve the brown sugar. Lower the heat and simmer for 10 to 15 minutes, to give the spices time to flavor the cider. Pour through a fine-mesh sieve into a carafe for serving or directly into warmed mugs. Garnish each drink with a cinnamon stick and serve.

BLACK CHERRY CIDER

Serves 4

2   cinnamon sticks

1   teaspoon whole allspice berries

1   teaspoon whole cloves

3   cups black cherry juice

1   cup apple cider

4   teaspoons sugar

3   tablespoons plain dried sour cherries (preferably unsweetened, with no oil added)

You can use cherry juice alone for this drink, but the apple cider gives the drink body and depth. Keep the spicing light and simple, so that the cherry flavor isn't overpowered.

Tie the cinnamon, allspice, and cloves in a cheesecloth bag and place in a medium saucepan. Pour in the juice and cider, then add the sugar and dried cherries. Bring to a boil over medium heat, then lower the heat and simmer for 5 minutes. Discard the spice bag and pour the cider into 4 mugs, spooning a few plumped cherries into each. Serve with spoons for the fruit.

HOT BENEFACTOR

Serves 2

2   teaspoons simple syrup
    (recipe follows), or 2
    teaspoons sugar plus 2
    teaspoons water
1   cup rum
1   cup red wine
2   slices lemon for garnish
    Freshly grated nutmeg
    for garnish

This super-easy drink is a great way to use wine left over from last night's dinner, and is one of the most truly warming drinks in this collection.

Put the simple syrup in a saucepan over medium heat, add the rum and wine, and bring just to a simmer. Pour into 2 warmed mugs, garnish with the lemon slices, and sprinkle with nutmeg. Serve immediately.

Makes 2 cups

2   cups sugar
2   cups water

Simple Syrup

Simple syrup can be used much like liquid cane syrup to sweeten hot or iced teas and coffees and cocktails.

Combine the water and sugar in a small saucepan over medium heat and bring to a boil, stirring to dissolve the sugar. Remove from the heat and let cool. Transfer to a very clean jar with a tight-fitting lid and store in the refrigerator; the syrup will keep for weeks.

HOT MILK PUNCH

Serves 2

1   cup whole milk
¾   cup brandy
2   teaspoons confectioners'
    sugar
1   very fresh large egg
    Dash of ground cinnamon
    Freshly grated nutmeg
    for garnish

This milk punch uses raw egg, so be sure to use very fresh and preferably pasteurized eggs. You also can omit the egg and add ¼ cup heavy cream to make up for the lost richness (though the drink won't be as foamy).

Put the milk, brandy, confectioners' sugar, egg, and cinnamon in a 2-quart nonstick saucepan and whisk to combine. Cook over very low heat until just steaming, about 3 minutes; watch the pan carefully, and remove from the heat as soon as the mixture is steaming and bubbles just begin to form at the edges of the pan. Immediately remove from the heat and whisk vigorously to create a thick foam on top of the milk. Pour into 2 warmed cups or mugs and dust the tops with nutmeg. Serve immediately.

DUTCH WARM MILK

Serves 2

2 cups whole milk
2 to 4 *Anijsblokjes*

If you're having trouble sleeping, or just want to wind down before bedtime, try this popular Dutch remedy: It'll make you absolutely catatonic.

Warm the milk in a small saucepan over low heat until the surface begins to quiver, but do not let it boil. Pour into 2 warmed mugs and stir 1 or 2 *anijsblokjes* into each.

Anijsblokjes (Anise Sugar Cubes)

I was told about anijsblokjes *at a party last winter, and I was eager to try them in warm milk. Unable to find them in stores, and unwilling to import them from Holland at great expense, I decided to make them myself.*

Makes about thirty-four 1-inch cubes or stars

½ cup sugar
⅛ teaspoon finely ground anise

Put the sugar in a mixing bowl and stir in the anise with a fork. Sprinkle the sugar mixture with 1¼ teaspoons cold water and stir well with the fork or your fingers until the sugar is evenly moistened. The sugar should resemble slightly dry sand castle–making sand. Pack the damp sugar into small plastic candy molds; this amount is enough to fill 2 sheets of 17 (1-inch) star-shaped molds each. Set aside in a cool place until completely dry and hard, about 3 hours. Turn the mold upside down and tap out the sugar stars. You can store them almost indefinitely in an airtight container.

Note: Plastic candy molds are available in good cookware stores or in baking-supply stores.

WARM BRANDY FLIP

Serves 2

½ cup brandy

1 very fresh large egg

1½ teaspoons simple syrup
(page 120)

½ cup whole milk

Freshly grated nutmeg
for garnish

This easy old-fashioned drink is a sure cure for mild insomnia. It does include raw egg, though, so be sure to use a fresh—and preferably pasteurized—egg.

In a blender, combine the brandy, egg, simple syrup, and milk. Blend on high speed until slightly frothy, about 1 minute. Transfer the mixture to a 2-quart nonstick saucepan. Cook over very low heat until just steaming, about 2 minutes; watch the pan carefully, and remove from the heat as soon as the mixture is steaming and bubbles just begin to form at the edges of the pan. (If you let it get too hot and the egg starts to cook, just pour the mixture back into the blender and blend again until smooth.) Pour into warmed highball glasses and dust with nutmeg. Serve immediately.

STUFFED DATES

About 24 large dates

½ Granny Smith apple, peeled, cored, and finely shredded

Juice of ½ lemon

3 ounces sharp cheddar cheese, finely shredded (about ½ cup)

½ cup toasted walnuts, chopped

2 tablespoons mayonnaise

1 teaspoon curry powder

½ teaspoon ground cayenne

½ teaspoon salt

These somewhat intensely flavored sweet-savory snacks could be served as cocktail-party snacks with strong rum drinks (hot or cold), or as an accompaniment to an afternoon pot of black Assam tea. Leftover filling can be spread thinly on chapatis or split pitas and broiled until bubbly; it will keep, tightly covered in the refrigerator, for several days.

Pit the dates, slitting one side lengthwise but keeping each date in one piece. Flatten them a bit so that they're cup-shaped.

In a medium bowl, combine all the remaining ingredients and stir to form a thick paste. Spoon teaspoonfuls of the mixture into the dates, mounding it up slightly. The dates can be stuffed and refrigerated, covered, the day before you plan to serve them; bring to room temperature before proceeding.

Preheat the broiler. Place the stuffed dates, filling side up, on a sheet pan and broil them, about 4 inches from the heat source, for 3 to 4 minutes, until the filling is bubbly and the dates are just starting to brown on top—watch them closely so they don't burn. Serve hot or at room temperature.

METRIC CONVERSION CHART

WEIGHT EQUIVALENTS

The metric weights given in this chart are not exact equivalents, but have been rounded up or down slightly to make measuring easier.

Avoirdupois	Metric
$\frac{1}{4}$ oz	7 g
$\frac{1}{2}$ oz	15 g
1 oz	30 g
2 oz	60 g
3 oz	90 g
4 oz	115 g
5 oz	150 g
6 oz	175 g
7 oz	200 g
8 oz ($\frac{1}{2}$ lb)	225 g
9 oz	250 g
10 oz	300 g
11 oz	325 g
12 oz	350 g
13 oz	375 g
14 oz	400 g
15 oz	425 g
16 oz (1 lb)	450 g
$1\frac{1}{2}$ lb	750 g
2 lb	900 g
$2\frac{1}{4}$ lb	1 kg
3 lb	1.4 kg
4 lb	1.8 kg

VOLUME EQUIVALENTS

These are not exact equivalents for American cups and spoons, but have been rounded up or down slightly to make measuring easier.

American	Metric	Imperial
$\frac{1}{4}$ t	1.2 ml	
$\frac{1}{2}$ t	2.5 ml	
1 t	5.0 ml	
$\frac{1}{2}$ T (1.5 t)	7.5 ml	
1 T (3 t)	15 ml	
$\frac{1}{4}$ cup (4 T)	60 ml	2 fl oz
$\frac{1}{3}$ cup (5 T)	75 ml	$2\frac{1}{2}$ fl oz
$\frac{1}{2}$ cup (8 T)	125 ml	4 fl oz
$\frac{2}{3}$ cup (10 T)	150 ml	5 fl oz
$\frac{3}{4}$ cup (12 T)	175 ml	6 fl oz
1 cup (16 T)	250 ml	8 fl oz
$1\frac{1}{4}$ cups	300 ml	10 fl oz ($\frac{1}{2}$ pt)
$1\frac{1}{2}$ cups	350 ml	12 fl oz
2 cups (1 pint)	500 ml	16 fl oz
$2\frac{1}{2}$ cups	625 ml	20 fl oz (1 pint)
1 quart	1 liter	32 fl oz

OVEN TEMPERATURE EQUIVALENTS

Oven Mark	F	C	Gas
Very cool	250-275	130-140	$\frac{1}{2}$ –1
Cool	300	150	2
Warm	325	170	3
Moderate	350	180	4
Moderately hot	375	190	5
	400	200	6
Hot	425	220	7
	450	230	8
Very hot	475	250	9

CREDITS & SOURCES

The following manufacturers and retailers generously provided equipment that was used in developing and testing the recipes contained in this book: All-Clad Metalcrafters; BonJour; Chicago Metallic Bakeware; Cuisinart; KitchenAid Home Appliances; Russell Hobbes, Waring Products, Inc., and Williams-Sonoma.

ALL-CLAD METALCRAFTERS LLC
424 Morganza Road
Canonsburg, Pennsylvania 15317
Toll free: 1 (900) 255-2523
www.allclad.com
Known for their fine cookware, All-Clad makes a beautiful coffee urn for serving a crowd; their 7-quart, stainless-steel slow cooker can also be found at Williams-Sonoma stores and Williams-Sonoma.com.

BONJOUR, INC.
80 Berry Drive
Pacheco, California 94553
Toll free: 1 (800) 2-bonjour (226-6568)
www.bonjourproducts.com
BonJour features a complete line of stovetop espresso pots, French press pots, and milk frothers, as well as beautiful teapots, infusers, and serving sets.

CHICAGO METALLIC, THE BAKEWARE COMPANY
120n Lakeview Parkway
Vernon Hills, Illinois 60061
www.bakingpans.com
The nonstick bakeware manufactured by Chicago Metallic makes for perfect baking and easy clean up.

CUISINART
Toll free: 1 (800) 726-0190
www.cuisinart.com
In addition to their famous food processors, look to Cuisinart for a full range of countertop appliances, including coffeemakers, burr grinders, and coffee grinders.

KALUSTYAN'S
123 Lexington Avenue
New York, New York 10016
Toll free: 1 (800) 352-3451
www.kalustyans.com
Kalustyan's, the anchor of Manhattan's Little Indian neighborhood, is one of my favorite stores in New York, and their website, though the online prices are slightly higher, features an excellent selection of spices and specialty foods—look here for palm sugar, special honeys, masala spice mixes, Assam teas, and fancy juices and syrups. The spices are fresh and reasonably priced.

KITCHENAID
Countertop Appliance Information
P.O. Box 218
St. Joseph, Michigan 49085
Toll free: 1 (800) 541-6390
www.kitchenaid.com
KitchenAid manufactures a complete range of appliances both large and small, including a complete line of coffeemakers, burr grinders, coffee grinders, and a countertop espresso machine.

PENZEYS SPICES
19300 West Janacek Court
Brookfield, Wisconsin 53008-0924
Toll-free: 1 (800) 741-7787
www.penzeys.com
This venerable mail-order spice purveyor's catalog is a cook's dream come true, and all of its products are available online. This is the place to order good Vietnamese cinnamon, arbol chiles, pure vanilla extract, and whole vanilla beans.

RUSSELL HOBBS

Toll-free: 1 (888) HOBBS-20 (462-2720)

www.russell-hobbs.com

Russell Hobbs offers electric teakettles in a range of beautiful designs, as well as coffeemakers, immersion blenders, and other countertop appliances.

SCHARFFEN BERGER

914 Heinz Avenue

Berkeley, California 94710

Toll free: 1 (800) 930-4528

www.scharffenberger.com

Scharffen Berger is a young chocolate company based in California. Their dark chocolates and couverture chocolates, natural cocoa powder, and cacao nibs are available online.

WARING PRODUCTS

314 Ella T. Grasso Avenue

Torrington, Connecticut 06790

Toll free: 1 (800) 4WARING (492-7464)

www.waringproducts.com

Specializing in blenders, the Waring line of countertop appliances includes juicers, drink mixers, coffeemakers, and an electric meat grinder.

WILLIAMS-SONOMA

3250 Van Ness Avenue

San Francisco, CA 94109

Toll-free: (877) 812-6235

www.williams-sonoma.com

There are more products available on the website of this fine-kitchen-wares retailer than the company features in its brick-and-mortar stores—look here for the very best espresso machines, burr grinders, milk frothers, blenders, silicone-coated whisks, other high-end appliances and kitchen utensils, and gourmet food products.

INDEX

A

Accompaniments
  biscotti, walnut-cherry, *91*, 92
  candies, chocolate-dipped orange, *41*, 42
  chocolates, crunchy espresso-bean, *102*, 103
  churros, *32*, 33
  dates, stuffed, 126
  lavender blossoms, candied, *69*, 70
  marshmallows, peppermint-stuffed, *20*, 28–29
  nuts, spiced candied, *115*, 116
  teacake, persimmon, *72*, 73
  turnovers, guava and *queso fresco*, *36*, 38–39
  whipped cream, barely sweetened, 34
Alcohol, coffee drinks with
  café brûlot, 100, 109
  coffee grog, 96, *97*, 109
  espresso, sweetened, with grappa, 101, *102*
  Irish coffee, real, 94
  penny rum, hot, 95
  Swiss coffee cocktail, *98*, 99
Alcohol, tea drinks with
  lychee black tea with cherry wine, *64*, 65
  sake and pear oolong tea, 66, *67*
  toddy, hot, 63
Alcohol-based drinks
  benefactor, hot, 120
  brandy flip, warm, *124*, 125
  buttered bourbon, hot, 114, *115*
  glügg, *106*, 109, 110
  milk punch, hot, 121
  mulled white wine with peach juice, 112, *113*
  mulled wine, 109, 111

Almond hot cocoa, 46
Anijsblokjes (anise sugar cubes), 122, *123*
Arbol chile hot cocoa, *36*, 37

B

Barley tea, 60, *61*
Basil-mint hot chocolate, 47
Benefactor, hot, 120
Biscotti, walnut-cherry, *91*, 92
Black peppercorn, persimmon
  & ginger tea, 71, *72*
Buttered bourbon, hot, 114, *115*

C

Cacao nib masa drink, *48*, 49
Café brûlot with cinnamon cream,
  100, 109
Cappuccino, basic, 88
Chai tea, basic, *50*, 58
Cherry
  black cherry cider, *118*, 119
  -walnut biscotti, *91*, 92
  wine, lychee black tea with, *64*, 65
Chicory coffee, 93
Chile-cinnamon infusion
  with dried jujubes, 74, *75*
Chile hot chocolate, *36*, 37
Chocolate and cocoa, hot
  INGREDIENTS, EQUIPMENT, TECHNIQUES,
  18–19, 22–26, *25*, 30
  almond cocoa, 46

arbol chile cocoa, *36*, 37

basic chocolate, *20*, 28

basic cocoa, 30

basil-mint chocolate, 47

cacao nib masa drink, *48*, 49

café mocha, 90, *91*

Earl Grey-scented chocolate, 35

4 A.M. in Madrid: *churros y chocolate*, 31–33, *32*

Mexican chocolate two ways, 44–45

orange-scented chocolate, 34

rose flower white chocolate, *2*, 43

saffron-orange white chocolate, 40, *41*

Chocolate-dipped orange candies, *41*, 42

Chocolates, crunchy espresso-bean, *102*, 103

Churros y chocolate, 31–33, *32*

Cider, black cherry, *118*, 119

Cider, classic mulled, 117

Cinnamon-chile infusion with dried jujubes, 74, *75*

Cocoa. See Chocolate and cocoa, hot

Coffee

INGREDIENTS, EQUIPMENT, TECHNIQUES, *9–11*, 9–12, 16–19, *17*, 78–86, 83

café brûlot, 100, 109

café mocha, 90, *91*

cappuccino, basic, 88

chicory coffee, 93

espresso, sweetened, with grappa, 101, *102*

grog, 96, *97*, 109

Irish coffee, real, 94

Koreatown Cuban coffee, *76*, 89

melya, 104, *105*

penny rum, hot, 95

Swiss coffee cocktail, *98*, 99

Coffee-and-chocolate drinks

café mocha, 90, 91

melya, 104, *105*

Cuban coffee, Koreatown, *76*, 89

D

Dates, stuffed, 126

Dutch warm milk, 122, *123*

E

Earl Grey-scented hot chocolate, 35

Espresso, sweetened, with grappa, 101, *102*

Espresso-bean chocolates, crunchy, *102*, 103

F

Flip, warm brandy, *124*, 125

4 A.M. in Madrid, 31–33, *32*

G

Garnishes. See Accompaniments

Ginger, persimmon & black peppercorn tea, 71, *72*

Glügg, *106*, 109, 110

Grappa, sweetened espresso with, 101, *102*

Grog, coffee, 96, *97*, 109

Guava and queso fresco turnovers, *36*, 38–39

H

Holiday spiced tea, 62

Honeyed tisane, 68, *69*

Hot drinks, to serve, 19, 108–9

I

Irish coffee, real, 94

J

Jujubes, dried, cinnamon-chile infusion with, 74, *75*

K

Koreatown Cuban coffee, *76*, 89

L

Lavender blossoms, candied, *69*, 70

Lychee black tea with cherry wine, *64*, 65

M

Marshmallows, peppermint-stuffed, *20*, 28–29

Masa cacao nib drink, *48*, 49

Melya, 104, *105*

Mexican hot chocolate, 44–45

Milk, Dutch warm, 122, *123*

Milk punch, hot, 121

Mint-basil hot chocolate, 47

Mocha café with coffee whipped cream, 90, *91*

Mulled cider, classic, 117

Mulled white wine with peach juice, 112, *113*

Mulled wine, 111

N

Nuts, spiced candied, *115*, 116

O

Orange

candies, chocolate-dipped, *41*, 42

-saffron white chocolate, 40, *41*

-scented hot chocolate, 34

P

Peach juice, mulled white wine with, 112, *113*

Pear and sake oolong tea, 66, *67*

Penny rum, hot, 95

Peppermint-stuffed marshmallows, *20*, 28–29

Persimmon, black peppercorn & ginger tea, 71, *72*

Persimmon teacake, *72*, 73

Q

Queso fresco and guava turnovers, *36*, 38–39

R

Rose flower white chocolate, *2*, 43

S

Saffron-orange white chocolate, 40, *41*

Sake and pear oolong tea, 66, *67*

Spiced tea, holiday, 62

Swiss coffee cocktail, *98*, 99

T

Tea

INGREDIENTS, EQUIPMENT, TECHNIQUES,
13–19, 52–57, *55–56*

basic chai, *50*, 58

cinnamon-chile infusion with dried
jujubes, 74, *75*

Earl Grey-scented hot chocolate, 35

green tea "cappuccino," 59

holiday spiced, 62

honeyed tisane, 68, *69*

lychee black, with cherry wine, 64, 65

persimmon, black peppercorn & ginger,
71, *72*

sake and pear oolong, 66, *67*

toasted barley, 60, *61*

toddy, hot, 63

Teacake, persimmon, *72*, 73

Tisane, honeyed, 68, *69*

Toddy, hot, 63

Turnovers, guava and queso fresco,
36, 38–39

W

Walnut-cherry biscotti, *91*, 92

Whipped cream, barely sweetened, 34

Wine, mulled, 109, 111

Wine, mulled white, with peach juice,
112, *113*

Edited by Marisa Bulzone
Designed by Julie Hoffer
Graphic Production by Norman Watkins
Prop Stylist: Lynda White
Food Stylist: Michael Pederson

The text of this book was composed in Granjon and Myriad